Jake Ferris
November 2017

Mary Jane Whiteley Coggeshall, Hicksite Quaker, Iowa/National Suffragette and Her Speeches

John N. (Jake) Ferris

Kids At Heart Publishing LLC
PO Box 492
Milton, IN 47357
765-478-5873
www.kidsatheartpublishing.com

First published by Kids At Heart Publishing LLC 5/16/2017
ISBN # 978-1-9461710-1-6
Library of Congress Control Number: 2017932157

Printed in the United States of America
Milton, Indiana

This book printed on acid-free paper.

The books at Kids At Heart Publishing feature turn the page technology.
No batteries or charging required.

Dedication

I dedicate this book to my parents, Albert and Elma Henby Ferris, who provided me the rich working experience of growing up on a family farm, and established an intellectual environment with emphasis on education. In particular, this book is dedicated to my mother, an Orthodox Quaker, who voted in the national election in 1920, the first year women could vote and the first time, at her age, she could vote. To my father, a Hicksite Quaker, politically conservative but liberal religiously, I am indebted to his Hicksite interpretation of the Bible.

About the Author

Born in 1929 and raised on a farm adjacent to Milton, Indiana, Jake Ferris pursued the field of agricultural economics with a BS from Purdue University, an MS from Cornell University and a PhD from Michigan State University, where he spent the remainder of his professional career. For 40 years he was a member of the Department of Agricultural, Food and Resource Economics blending extension, on-campus teaching, international programs, research and consulting with emphasis on agricultural price analysis, outlook and marketing strategies. He wrote monthly articles on the agricultural outlook for *The Michigan Farmer* and *The National Livestock Producer* for a number of years.

The second printing of the second edition of his graduate textbook, *Agricultural Prices and Commodity Market Analysis*, first published by WCB McGraw Hill in 1998 and now distributed by the Michigan State University Press, was released in 2011. After retirement from Michigan State University in 1997, as a professor emeritus, he consulted with a private agricultural market news firm based in Chicago on biofuels for 10 years. Among his awards were the "1996 Distinguished Service to Agriculture Award" from the Michigan Farm Bureau and the "Certificate of Distinction for Outstanding Service to Agriculture" from the Purdue Agricultural Alumni Association in 2007.

A birthright Quaker, he retained his basic faith as a "Hicksite" although a member of another protestant church. Loving history prompted him to write a genealogy of the Ferris family. In this research, he became fascinated by the Iowa and national roles of, and the accolades given to suffragette Mary Jane Whiteley Coggeshall, sister of his great grandmother, Lydia Whiteley Ferris.

Acknowledgments

For over 30 years, Cynde Coggeshall Fanter, great granddaughter of Mary Jane Whiteley Coggeshall, has provided this author, from time to time, with intriguing information about her remarkable ancestor. Ann Delong Haase, Cynde's first cousin and also a great granddaughter of Mary Janes's, filled the gap of information on the employment of John Milton Coggeshall, Mary Janes's husband. The very extensive genealogy of *The Whiteley Family* by Mary Catherine Sample reflected her careful inspection of Quaker meeting records supplemented by numerous interviews and photos. Her book was an invaluable source. Credit also goes to Lydia Whiteley Ferris who kept records of her family, letters and other mementos. Of course, the CD of MJC's speeches from the Schlesinger Library, Radcliffe Institute, Harvard University and the help received on site made this book possible. Anna Stanton, first cousin of MJC's, wrote an autobiography which not only records the role of Hicksite Quakers in educating African Americans after the Civil War, it included insights on Mary Jane and her family. Tom Hamm, Professor of History at Earlham College, has had valuable input into this book and graciously supplied a foreword. Finally, this author wishes to thank his wife, Maxine Schnitzer Ferris, for editing the manuscript. She is an excellent editor, a skill for which she is professionally trained.

Foreword

Perhaps no religious group in American history has exercised such influence in proportion to numbers than has the Religious Society of Friends, or Quakers. They rose during the English Revolution of the 1640s and 1650s, the only one of the numerous radical groups that emerged from the unsettlement of those years. In North America, they played a variety of roles in the English colonies. In New England and the Chesapeake, they were an irritation to established churches and duly constituted authorities, so much so that Massachusetts authorities actually hanged four. Where they acquired power, as in Pennsylvania, they saw themselves as engaged in a "Holy Experiment," trying to prove to the world that a society could be founded, and flourish, on foundations of religious liberty, peace, and justice for all people, regardless of race.

That idealism led Friends, beginning in the 1750s, to engage the larger society around them as philanthropists and reformers. They began by defending the rights of Native Americans engaged in treaty negotiations. By 1800 they had also become leaders in movements ranging from prison reform to humane treatment of the mentally ill. Quakers were most identified in the public mind, however, with opposition to slavery. A few Friends had expressed qualms about slaveholding in the seventeenth century. When a broad antislavery movement emerged in North America and Western Europe after 1750, Quakers like John Woolman and Anthony Benezet were central to it. When the American Anti-Slavery Society formed in Philadelphia in 1833, at least a third of its founders were Friends.

One of the peculiarities that distinguished Friends from the beginning was their embrace of public roles for women. Almost alone among their contemporaries, Quakers believed that women had as much right as men to be ministers, to preach and pray publicly. Quaker business affairs were conducted by parallel structures at all levels of men and women. Thus it is unsurprising that when the first women's rights convention in American history was held at Seneca Falls, New York, in the summer of 1848, four of the five organizers were Quaker women. Of the three major figures in the women's rights movement in the United States before 1900, Lucretia Mott, Elizabeth Cady Stanton, and Susan B. Anthony, Mott and Anthony were Friends.

Three years after the Seneca Falls convention, in October 1851, the first women's rights convention in Indiana was held in the small town of Dublin in Wayne County. We have no way of knowing now whether a resident of the nearby town of Milton, Mary Jane Whiteley, born in 1836, knew of what was happening a few miles to the north. But as she reached adulthood, and after her marriage to John M. Coggeshall, Mary Jane Coggeshall would become firmly committed to the cause of women's rights. Like many Hoosiers who came of age in the years before the Civil War, she moved west in 1865, spending the rest of her life in Iowa. There she would devote her talents to the cause of equality for women. Although revered by fellow feminists in her day, and called "my greatest inspiration" by no less a women's rights icon than Carrie Chapman Catt, she has been largely forgotten. Thus we should be grateful to her great grand nephew, Jake Ferris, for this reconstruction of her life and times.

Thomas D. Hamm

Professor of History
Earlham College

Contents

Introduction

The national and state woman suffrage movement in the U.S. has its roots in the anti-slavery movement in 1840. In June of that year, a meeting known as the World's Anti-Slavery Convention was held in London, England. Six women were elected in the U.S. to attend the conference. They were rejected because (1) Anti-slavery leaders did not want women's rights issues to dilute the focus of the convention; and (2) The social mores of the time generally prohibited women's participation in public political life (Wikipedia, "Lucretia Mott").

Two of the six women were Lucretia Coffin Mott and Elizabeth Cady Stanton. Upon returning to America, they vowed to organize a conference on women's rights, which they did in Seneca Falls, NY in July 1848. Mott, a Hicksite Quaker, and Stanton had the assistance of three other local female Quakers. This county was populated by Hicksite Quakers, most likely the reason for the Seneca Falls location (Wikipedia, "Seneca Falls Convention").

Actually, woman suffrage was not on Mott's agenda; and she opposed the enfranchisement resolution which passed by a large majority. Frederick Douglas, the only African American at the meeting, stood and spoke eloquently in favor of the resolution. A former slave, he became a national leader in abolition, and as a statesman, was noted for his oratory and writing.

Following the Seneca Falls convention, two national organizations emerged in 1869 -- the National Woman Suffrage Association (NWSA) and the American Woman Suffrage Association (AWSA) (Wikipedia, "Women's Suffrage in the United States"). Heading NWSA were Susan B. Anthony and Stanton and others. Heading the NWSA were Lucy Stone, Julia Ward Howe, Henry Blackwell (Stone's husband) and others. Alice Stone Blackwell, daughter of Lucy Stone and Henry Blackwell (Lucy retained her maiden name), was a major influence in bringing the rival suffrage leaders together, proposing a joint meeting in 1887. The merger to become the National American Woman Suffrage Association (NAWSA) was accomplished in 1890.

Carrie Chapman Catt began working for the NAWSA's Iowa association in 1890 and also for the national association (Wikipedia, "Carrie Chapman Catt"). She was even a speaker at its 1890 convention in Washington, DC. In 1892, Susan B. Anthony asked Catt to address Congress on the woman's suffrage amendment. Catt would succeed Anthony as NAWSA president, being elected from 1900 to 1904 and in 1915.

Mary Jane Whiteley Coggeshall, the subject of this book, became a suffragette in Des Moines, IA in 1870, five years after leaving Milton, IN. The later connection with Catt's involvement with the NAWSA in Iowa in 1890 likely became the reason Coggeshall was added to the board of the NAWSA in 1895. Catt cited Coggeshall as "The Mother of Woman Suffrage in Iowa" and "my greatest inspiration." Moreover, a most glowing compliment to Coggeshall after she died in 1911 came from Alice Stone Blackwell who brought the rival associations together in 1890.

Mary Jane Whiteley Coggeshall was born on January 17, 1836 on a farm near Milton, Indiana and died in Des Moines, IA on December 22, 1911. On November 10, 1857, she married John Milton Coggeshall. Because she was a member of the Hicksite branch of the Quaker meeting in Milton and he was a member of the Orthodox branch north of Milton, they were both disowned by their branches. Later, both became members of the Orthodox branch by condemning their misconduct. However, Mary Jane continued to hold strong beliefs with the Hicksites even after joining the Des Moines Unitarian Church in 1886 when an ardent suffragist became the minister (Gordon, 2008). Mary Jane was prominently connected with Iowa and national women's suffrage movement for 41 years (Sample, 1986). In 1990, she was inducted, posthumously, into the Iowa Women's Hall of Fame as "the mother of woman suffrage in Iowa."

Accolades to M.J. Coggeshall

Before presenting the collection of Coggeshall's speeches, a section of the tributes to her is included here from the "Genealogy of the Ferris Family of Milton, Indiana" (Ferris, John, 2010). The Coggeshalls moved to Des Moines, IA in 1865 in a covered wagon when Mary Jane was 29 years of age and he was about 36. We have not been able to establish the reasons for this move. Our first recognition of the role Mary Jane played in the suffrage movement was the heading on the stationery of a letter to her sister Lydia Whiteley Ferris. The letter was dated June 21, 1902 as follows:

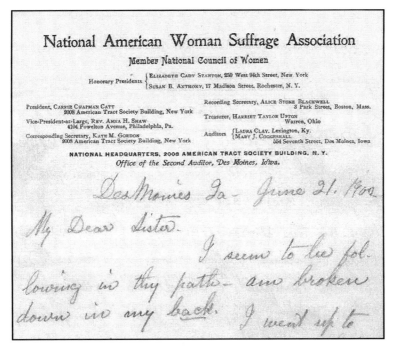

Fig. 1 Beginning of a letter to Lydia Whiteley Ferris from her sister, Mary Jane Whiteley Coggeshall. Note her prominence in the National American Woman Suffrage Association where she had been on the board since 1895 (Source: Ferris, Lydia Whiteley).

In this very newsy letter about family, Mary Jane added, "I am almost ashamed of these letterheads. A great amount of them — with envelopes were sent me from N. York (had to pay dollar expressage). I do not like them, but suppose because I am the tail end of the Auditing Committee, I am entitled to them."

Mary Jane's tribute to Susan B. Anthony at the memorial service at the Central Church of Christ in Des Moines, Iowa on March 15, 1906 deserves quotation in its entirety. Her remarks follow:

> As King David said to his servants, "Surely a great man and a prophet has this day fallen in Israel," she to whom we bring tribute today was a prophet of better things to be; one who has turned the whole tide of human convictions. She came upon the stage when slavery was practiced in almost every land and all women were under the ban of customs that were relics of barbarism. If achievements can measure the length of life, Miss Anthony has lived a thousand years.

Born into the spiritual freedom of the Hicksite Quaker Church, independent of all things save the inner light like the Apostle Paul "after the way they call heresy," worshipped she the God of her fathers. Early putting aside what woman holds most dear in a home of her own. Not for her the sweet companionship of a husband, not for her the gentle clasp of baby fingers. She threw her whole splendid genius into making the world a better place to live in.

The mother who takes into her heart her own children may be a very ordinary woman, but she who takes into her heart the children of a nation is one of God's mothers. The ancient philosophy was wrong which taught that men and women were made heroes by becoming indifferent to life and death. Men and women are made heroes by loving something more than life or death, and Miss Anthony has given to the cause of humanity, and especially the cause of woman, every year, every month, every day and every hour of her life.

Her sublime faith in the final triumph of right made failure impossible. She counted every defeat as but a milestone to victory, and over and over has her cheerful sympathy been poured out to the women of Iowa as we have counted our milestones --- a sympathy that is painfully fresh in our memories.

As the years went by she grew in love and saintly patience. Sometimes when she was sorely tried with the emptiness of the legislators and the stolidity of congressmen, when other women would grow impatient and indignant at the delay, then this seer among the daughters of men would come among us, saying: "Remember, sisters, that these men are born of subject mothers. They are all the sons of bond-woman and in spite of themselves they have the bond-woman's legacy."

It is said that to be the great reformer that he leaves his work incomplete -- creates desires which he cannot satisfy. So with Miss Anthony; and it was the great satisfaction of the last twenty years of her life that there had come to her a vast army of women yearly increasing in numbers who walk by the same rule and mind the same thing. She felt that her

4

going away would be no more than a gentle ripple stirring the ripening grain.

Brave, courageous, loving, Miss Anthony --- as was said of another --- "She came into the world crying while all about her laughed — she left the world smiling while all about her wept."

The "forwardness" of Mary Jane Whiteley Coggeshall can be detected in the following letter on the stationery of the Iowa Woman Suffrage Association, dated March 29, 1895 (Fanter, 2002).

My Dear Mrs. Hooper,

I write to invite you to join us in a raid upon the business men of Des Moines next Tuesday. The plan is to meet at the Kirkwood, at say nine o'clock, leave home for the whole day, and all are most cordially invited to dine with me at my ?? restaurant.

We can go by twos, in the thickest & best part of the City, and where the walking will be least, and make as big a demonstration as we can --- and then go home in the evening & try to forget whatever may have been disagreeable. We can ask our men friends (& we do have some) to show their faith by their works --- to give us fifty cents & become members of our society. We would doubtless have some rare experiences to relate at the meeting Thursday. If we can one day, and make a kind of picnic of it, perhaps we can live over it.

Cordially,
M. J. Coggeshall

If you think you can come please send me a card.

A special "Women's Edition of the Register and Leader" on women's suffrage was published in Des Moines, IA on May 12, 1915 (The Des Moines Register, 1915). Prominent in this edition was a picture of Mary Jane Coggeshall and an article as follows:

Mrs. Coggeshall was in the center of the suffrage movement in Iowa for more than forty years. She was one of the early presidents of the Iowa Equal Suffrage Association and served in this capacity many times. For the last years of her life she was annually elected honorary president. She was a member of the board of the National Association and her advice and counsel had weight for many years in national affairs. She counted all the national leaders among her friends; and her beautiful character and personality have been an inspiration to many of the younger workers in Iowa, while she was a tower of strength to the hosts of friends of her own generation.

Fig. 2 Mary Jane Whiteley Coggeshall promoted woman suffrage for 41 years. Carrie Chapman Catt called her "The Mother of Woman Suffrage in Iowa" and "my greatest inspiration." (Source: Women's Edition of the Register and Leader, May 12, 1915).

A most glowing compliment in an article by Alice Stone Blackwell, President, Massachusetts' "Equal Suffrage Association" and daughter of Lucy Stone was this statement:

Mrs. Coggeshall, who lived until a few years ago, and is remembered with much affection, had not only wisdom and integrity, but a sweetness of character that made her face like an alabaster vase with a lamp inside it --- the light shone through. She had also a delicious gift of humor, and even in her old age was a more acceptable public speaker than most of the younger women. Again and again at the national suffrage conventions, I have seen that tall, slender white-haired lady, the mother of "eighteen feet of boys," as she used to say with pride --- stand on the platform and keep the great assembly in one continuous gale of laughter, all through her speech.

Strong as were the efforts of Anthony, Stanton, Coggeshall and many others before and at the turn of the century into the 1900s, it was not until 1920 that women were given the right to vote in federal elections. But as Susan B. Anthony promised, "Failure is Impossible."

Mary Jane Coggeshall is also recognized as a noted Des Moines resident. The picture in Figure 3 was taken in May 2005 at a rest stop on I-80 east of Des Moines with Jake Ferris's salutation. (Author's note: Rather than using first person singular, subsequent reference to the author will continue to be his nickname Jake.)

Fig. 3 State of Iowa Historical Society marker on I-80 east of Des Moines.

A Personal Note

Jake's mother, Elma Henby Ferris, voted in the national election in 1920, the first time she could vote and the first time women could vote. This puts the date into the classification of recent history.

Jake's great grandmother, Lydia Whiteley Ferris, sister of Mary Jane Whiteley Coggeshall, was also a suffragette. Her granddaughter Elizabeth Ferris Mills described the only time she saw her angry or perhaps very much upset. She was getting signers to a petition to allow a measure on woman suffrage to be brought to a vote. One man she approached, spit and shifted his wad of tobacco to the other cheek and drawled, "Well, Lydia, I don't think womens has got enough sense to vote." As Elizabeth described it, "She came home acting just like my little song sparrow when other birds invaded her territory" (Mills, 1947).

Organization of the remainder of the book

The translation of Mary Jane Coggeshall's 18 speeches forms the body of the book, plus her compilation of 155 responses from editors to her brief letter sent in 1882 asking their position on woman suffrage. Following are sections with more reflections on her career, suffrage memorabilia, John Milton Coggeshall and family, the Hicksite Quaker heritage, close Whiteley-Ferris family connection, and final tributes to Mary Jane Whiteley Coggeshall.

Translations of Speeches from Handwritten Copies

A CD with handwritten copies of the speeches of Mary Jane Whiteley Coggeshall was obtained in 2012 from the Arthur and Elizabeth Schlesinger Library on the History of Women in America at Radcliffe Institute connected to Harvard University in Cambridge, Massachusetts (Schlesinger Library, 2012). The bulk of the papers was given to the Schlesinger Library in 1946 by Coggeshall's granddaughter, Helen Coggeshall (Lingenfelter) Gray. Additional materials were given to the library by Helen Gray in 1983. The collection was reprocessed and microfilmed as part of a Schlesinger Library/University Publications of America. The microfilm was converted to a CD and the contents printed.

Jake did donate to the Library an original letter from Mary Jane Whiteley Coggeshall to his great grandmother, Lydia Whiteley Ferris (The first page is in the heading of Figure 1). Another addition was a picture of the Coggeshall home in Des Moines.

Some of the handwriting of Coggeshall was difficult to translate. Jake did add quite a bit of punctuation to help the reader. If a word was illegible, he inserted a blank. If not sure of a word, (?) was added. A visit to the Schlesinger Library in August 2016 enabled him to fill in many blanks from the CD and add to his collection. Yes, there is some duplication in her speeches, but these are relatively minor.

Impressive was Mary Jane's vocabulary. Jake found himself reaching for the dictionary frequently to see if the word existed (a few did not). She was also well versed in history and the Bible. As far as Jake knows, her education was not beyond high school, although Fanter mentions that she was a teacher before marrying Coggeshall at age 21 (Fanter, 2012). Also amazing was raising "eighteen feet of boys" plus a daughter. A son and daughter died before they left Milton in 1865 and a son died at the age of nine after they arrived in Des Moines, IA. One of her "eighteen feet of boys" drowned.

Curious as to the material which, as Alice Stone Blackwell claimed, kept "the great assembly in one continuous gale of laughter, all through her speech," Jake was somewhat disappointed that such was missing. Mary Jane must have had a separate joke book. One can get some indication of her sense of humor in the final two speeches included here (Portland, Oregon and "Then and Now").

Parts of her speeches are a bit difficult to interpret and can be skimmed. But please capture the breadth and intensity of this remarkable woman in her views on women's rights which received high praise from her colleagues and audiences.

The White Cross and Women's Purity (ca. 1886)

In Great Britain in sundry garrison towns there has been in operation for twenty years up to last November, a law known as the "Contagious Diseases Acts," which had made the virtue of English women and girls as legally an article of barter, and sale as the traffic in sugar and coffee.

The friends of Social Purity in England in an organization of which, Mrs. Josephine Butler is the inspired leader, -- a noble woman, who, as she sat in her darkened home from which her own lovely daughter had gone out forever – the call came to her that other mothers whose daughters had gone down to (their fate), however than the grave were suffering more than herself, so she gathered the friends together and for seventeen years have they worked and prayed, petitioned and waited for the repeal of this odious law. The horrible revelations made by the Pall Mall Gazette in 1885 so aroused the public conscience to the enormity of evil existing among them that, at last, the slow going English Parliament, with the approval of the Queen, cleansed the statute books of Great Britain of this terrible stain.

Growth of this English "Federation for the Preservation of State Regulated Vice," was the White Cross Movement in America.

An institution guided by the Rev. Dr. B. F. De Costa, D.D., of New York, the third anniversary of which was held in that city in February last. This movement has now spread into every state and territory of the Union, and has received the endorsement of the Episcopal Church at it's Triennial Session in Chicago, and it's scope enlarged by the seven methods of the clergy's official "Declaration" which has already been approved by nearly fifty of the Bishops.

Multitudes of men and women prominent in all circles, and professions, and refreshingly all classes of Christians, have given it their approval.

What is the White Cross Movement? It means a higher life for the individual, the church, and the Nation. Its object is increased purity, and it aims especially for a single moral standard for men and for women.

It asks the Church in all its branches to maintain this standard and by practice as well as precept; let the world know that what is sin in the woman, is sin in the man. In the world a double standard prevails today, the woman being condemned while the man, often, goes free.

The object of this movement to defeat bad legislation – legislation which purposes to make it safe for men to practice crimes against women.

Legislation that would set apart a certain class for the permanently degraded, for the use of men, the White Cross Society is formed for men alone, no woman or girl has even made a member. It is not a secret organization, and has no admission fee.

Each member takes this pledge:

I promise by the help of God to treat all women with respect and endeavor to protect them from wrong and degradation.

To endeavor to put down all indecent language and coarse jests.

To maintain the law of purity as equally binding upon men and women.

To endeavor to spread these principles among my companions and to try and help my companions, and to try to help my younger brothers.

To use every possible means to fulfill the command, "Keep thyself _____."

What has it already done!

It has been represented before legislative bodies to secure good laws, and to repeal bad ones.

It has already destroyed 36,000 lbs. of books – letter press – and 25,000 lbs. of electric and stereotype plates – 232,000 obscene pictures, 90,000 articles of immoral use – over one million obscene circulars and songs, and we must remember that these tons of matter destroyed is not a tithe of what goes into circulation.

Two hundred and seven books have been suppressed, 8 ½ tons of gambling implements were seized, and the addresses of 982,000 persons, for whom immoral literature was intended. In the annual report, the President says that "Few persons would be willing to believe the whole truth regarding these things."

The awful uses to which young girls, poor girls, are being put in this city (N. York) cannot be named, or even hinted at. That the degradation of women that now obtains is equaled, perhaps, only by the shocking indifference of men to the whole subject. Mrs. Josephine Rutter's large experience has taught her (Author's note: Five handwritten lines are missing).

The Rev. W.J. Sabine before the N. York Committee of this Society said, "I have reason to believe that many of my brethren in the ministry are in the utter darkness upon this matter." If this be true of this very intelligent body of Christians, what can we expect is the condition of other classes.

How many of us have been well informed upon this matter? I confess my own ignorance of the fact that there was any "age of consent" in this or any other state, until one year ago, when our wide-awake and vigilant sister of the "Women's Christian Temperance Union," brought the subject prominently before the people of the state.

This Social Purity movement by women is literally breaking a way through an untracked forest. A forest, black with an over-shadowing pall of ignorance which woman has ever been told she must not lift. Draw not the curtain aside – disturb not the dragons.

Have we not always understood that law is the perfection of reason! And our lawmakers sitting in the councils of state where no mother's voice is ever heard, have deliberately established decrees which today are on the statute books of eighteen states of the Union, by which, a man of any age has the right to use all the blandishments and persuasions that he can command upon your little girl or mine if she has passed her tenth birthday, and if he can so prevail over her ignorance or her fears as to yield to him her childish virtue – unless she or her friends can prove that she resisted him to the limit.

But the law-making power of this one-sexed government is as much out of harmony as a one sexed home. This law of "consent" virtually says, "Throw our white lambs to the vultures," for a court of justice in a neighboring state lately decided that it could not punish a fiendish libertine because "the most of his victims were over ten years of age."

Mrs. Helen Campbell's recently published articles in the New York Tribune entitled, "Prisoners of Poverty," turn for us a calcium light upon the indignities and perils to which great numbers of dependent women and girls are exposed. She says; "The woman's and the young and comely girl's extremity is the sensual man's opportunity." Three girls were once found in the maternity ward of a New York hospital, all giving the name of the same man who had brought them to deep distress and who was the foreman in the factory where they all worked. Jo Howard in the Boston Globe says of the 10,000 girls who stand behind the counter of the retail stores of that city, receiving an average of $3.50 a week, with an enforced vacation for many of them for six or eight weeks in which they get nothing; that out of this they are expected to clothe themselves respectably, pay car fare, doctor's bills, etc. He asks if this is a promenade on which can be placed the tender feet of girls too young to realize the snares that wait for them, but old enough to want to dress as well as their companions

Labor saving machinery and an ever increasing throng of unskilled applicants have so reduced wages that thousands of women are working like slaves for the privilege of starving. Do you say let them enter domestic service? This says Mrs. Campbell is not free from the same perils, and she gives cumulative testimony to show how strong must that dependent girl be to resist the persuasions and inducement to betrayal by the master or the son maybe. One mother whose fifteen year old daughter had been thus betrayed said; "I'll warn every girl to keep herself and learn a trade, and not run the risk she'll run if she goes out to service letting alone the way you're looked down on."

Miss Ellice Hopkins of Brighton, England to whom the cause of Social Purity in this country is greatly indebted makes this startling declaration; "Stop the money of men and the whole thing would be starved out in six weeks." Women are decoyed into dens of vice in the midst of thriving populations, into lonely towns on the frontier or taken out of the country altogether. It states that a woman well known to the Newark detectives brings young girls to Newark from New York two or three times a week, chiefly Germans and Jewesses, and sells them to the keepers of various houses. The commission being ten dollars a girl where they are accepted.

Recently in New York City was unearthed a system of traffic in women by which under promise of lawful work and good wages frequent installments of them were shipped to the Isthmus of Panama. With the procurer in New York and one at the Isthmus, and the proprietors of certain steamships all in collusion, the way was made easy and apparently most respectable, and innocent women – even women of mature years – were caught by the fair promises held out, and, once there, return was difficult and death in a very few months in that climate almost certain; and as De Leon, the New York procurer boasted, "dead women tell no tales." It is gratifying to know that a measure of justice has at last overtaken him, and he has been sentenced to fifteen years in the state prison.

And have not all our hearts been made to bleed for that frail seventeen years old girl who, alone in the cold and darkness on a wind-swept corner of the street in Chicago, became a mother? But stern law that knows no sex among its violators, lodges her in jail to answer to the crime of infanticide while the guilty partner to this tragedy holds high his scoundrel head among the ways of men.

Let a woman known to be a nymph walk down the street of a city and how many amorous eyes will take note of her steps; and we will say that she has lured our young men to ruin. Let a man known to be a libertine through and through walk down the same street, he will perhaps catch not one sensuous glance. No wonder that men are tempted of women when scores of them are lying in wait for just this opportunity. But does anyone suppose that in the sight of Heaven the woman is the greater sinner? It is estimated that for every licentious woman there are at least ten licentious men. Chicago is said to have 30,000 prostituted women. Think of 300,000 men in one city leading licentious lives. We may talk of female chastity, as long as we please, it cannot be without male chastity. But remembering that while our laws and the customs of society are thus lenient towards the lusts and passions of the stronger sex, let us never cease to thank God that notwithstanding these things are there yet in the world of so many pure men.

What can we do? Much, very much. But the speakers who are to follow me doubtless will get us out of the plenitude of their careful study, practical suggestions that will help women and thus humanity in its upward climb. While we would ask for woman that she be made a workman complete in building up the broken walls of our pain, yet each may with the help of God, single-handed and alone put every day a stone in the wall opposite her own door. She may first be pure and true herself and then begin to influence for purity her boys and girls while they are beneath the home roof – better even to begin while they are yet about her knees. Better still to begin twenty years before it is born.

Thus far we have spoken of prostitution only as it exist outside of marriage. Shall we speak of prostitution as it exists inside of marriage? And shall we not here find the Arch dragon – centuries old? Dare we stir him up! If humanity had no other guide, the ruder orders of nature might at last teach us that the female during gestation should be free from all passional interference. Ever since the earth brought forth beasts and birds and creeping things, these lower orders of creation have been the objects of the All-Fathers peculiar care. The female mastodon whose gigantic male made the primeval forests tremble beneath his tread was herself safe under that instinctive law that made her body inviolate. The lioness rests in her liar in quiet and serenity, even the covey which area a feeble folk gambol with its fellows, or seeks its burrow in security; throughout the whole animal creation, from the greatest to the least, the female is not only safe from interference during gestation, but she alone dictates when, or whether maternity shall be.

But what of the woman? Are ye not of more value than many sparrows?

I believe you will agree with me that in all human experience there is nothing so costly as an idea. We are now nearing the open door of the twentieth century and through all the growing ages has run the great unwritten law that the daughters of our sinning first mother have not the right to the complete control of their own persons. That highest and finest product of civilization – the monogamous marriage, Alas! Alas! How has it been defiled?

Mrs. Lucinda B. Chandler, President of the Moral Educational Society of Chicago, tells of a cultivated woman who from various causes had been whelmed in this final catastrophe of prostitution, when asked by her physician why she did not cease that mode of life and marry, as she was attractive enough to secure a good husband replied, "Marry! No, indeed! If I am sick or tired, or want to be alone, now, I have but to turn the key in that door, and no man has the right to demand entrance to my room, or the use of my body." This arraignment does not lose aptness or force because there are <u>many</u> comfortable and happy unions, where mutual respect and love make blessed and good the legal relations.

If through woman the world lost in Eden, was it not more than restored at Bethlehem? And forever blessed be the story of the Christ Mother, who, though Joseph was her husband, beloved yet he knew her not through all the hallowed days of their loving care of the Christ in _____. God was with Joseph as well as with Mary, and he has not forgotten the world, and we believe that earth is later Savior's will be thus tenderly guarded. Victor Hugo says: "He who has seen the misery of men only, has seen nothing. He must see the misery of women only, has seen nothing. He must see the misery of childhood."

We are glad when our children by the spirit of God moving upon them, are born the second time; but we believe the very angels in Heaven sing praises when a child comes to earth well born first time. And if women are appointed by God to be the conservators of the race, the world will work upward no faster than her feet shall clinch the heights of progress; and in these _____ days of peace the call comes to her most loudly – O! Woman! Rise and shine, for the glory of the Lord is risen upon thee!

But the property of every young girl in the land is surrounded with legal safe-guards so that she could not squander it if she would, before she is of legal age.

Georgia Mark, in the Union Signal, shows that by tracing back the old Common Law of England through its modifications to the present time there never has been a period in English history when girlish innocence was so early left unprotected by law as at the present.

Our country needs better protection for girls. It is a maxim of Mr. Gladstone "that it is the province of government to make it easy to do right and difficult to do wrong."

Social Purity (Read before the Polk County W.S.A.)

(Author's note: This paper was in print and in the possession of Lydia Whiteley Ferris, sister of Mary Jane Whiteley Coggeshall. Because the topic is similar to the previous speech on "The White Cross and women's purity," we would presume the date to be around 1886.)

Mrs. President, Members of the Woman's Suffrage Association, and Friends:

I was requested at the last meeting of this society to present a paper upon the slavery of women to the great social vice of the world.

Leaving out of this discussion the heathen nations and their practices, we find enough of social degradation in the civilized and Christian world to cause every woman's heart to sink before the appalling picture. Through the long and dreary ages out of the darkness of which we are just emerging, so dominant has been this master passion in man that the historian, Lecky, coolly records that the virtuous woman is safe only at the expense of a pariah class. Out of this base and fiendish doctrine has come as a natural result the effort to license its practice, and that half of humanity which holds the law-making power in its hands, has seen fit to make the traffic in the bodies of women, and the police and medical supervision of them, as lawful as the trading on sugar or salt.

This system of white slavery has existed in continental Europe for many years; it was instituted in France under the first Napoleon, late in the eighteenth century, and was introduced into Great Britain by act of parliament between 1866 and 1869. As a necessary accompaniment to the establishment of houses of prostitution under patronage of government, there exist all over the world an extensive traffic in this vice. All around the globe, and up and down our great highways of commerce, may be seen the sad procession of these youthful victims of human cruelty. Throughout the whole of Europe, especially in Germany and Austria, the exportation of white slaves is conducted on a large scale.

Mrs. Josephine Butler, of England, the leader in the formation of the "International Federation for the Abolition of the State Regulation of Vice," in her report to the International council at Washington, says; "numbers of those victims are embarked at Hamburg, whose destination is South America, Rio de Janeiro, Montevideo, and Buenos Aires. Others by the Straits of Magellan to Valparaiso. Other cargoes are sent to North America, sometime descending the Mississippi to New Orleans and Texas. In the market of California they are sorted and sent to provision the different localities on the coast as far as Panama. Others go from the New Orleans market to Cuba, the Antilles and Mexico. Other are taken from Germany, Bohemia and Switzerland, across the Alps to Italy and south to

Alexandria and Suez; eastward to Bombay and Shanghai. The Russian official houses of vice draw their slaves largely from eastern Prussia, Pomerania and Poland. The most important station is Riga. It is there that the traders of St. Petersburg and Moscow sort out and get ready their cargoes of women for Nijni-Novgorod, and from this place they are sent on to the more distant towns of Siberia, the victims being sometimes sold and resold in the long passage. But perhaps the strangest and saddest spectacle in all Christendom may be seen in one of the great trade arteries of London, the Whitechapel Road, where sexual vice is the chief industry of the population, and where hundreds upon hundreds of your sisters and mine walk the streets from dark to daylight, with no home, seldom sleeping twice under the same roof; and since the recent revolting murders in the district the police are ordered to rout them from their slumbers in stairways and cellars, and they are obliged to tramp about all night and all the next day until they can get fourpence to hire a bed."

But in our own beloved land with its blood-bought freedom from Negro slavery we find even here the servitude of woman assumes a blackness beside which southern slavery seems almost a worthy institution. In all our great cities like New York, St. Louis, Chicago, Cincinnati and others, thousands of women haunt the streets at night as their chief business in earning a livelihood; a careful estimate placing the general proportion of the whole number in the United States to be one for every fifty-two adult males.

It has come to the ears of authorities at Washington, that terrible wrongs are committed upon the native women of Alaska through the agents of employees of the Alaska Seal Fur Company. The poor Indians, having lost all patience, have addressed an appeal to the people of the United States for protection from the passions of these unprincipled white men. Senator Dawes has introduced into Congress a resolution "calling on the Secretary of the Interior for information, and whether steps have been taken by the department to protect these Indian women."

But in the discussion today, I wish to call your attention especially to the present outrages in the great "new north" of Wisconsin and Michigan. There, there exists a systematic organization of intelligent business men, which has for its object the amassing of fortunes by trading in the virtue of young women. In obtaining these facts I am greatly indebted to the report of Dr. Kate Bushnell, evangelist of the "White Cross and White Shield," and who was commissioned by the W.C.T.U. of Wisconsin to ascertain the facts concerning the notorious dens of this region, and who spent about four months of last year in the investigation. After the attention of Governor Rusk of Wisconsin, had been urgently called to the matter, he sent a detective to the northern part of the state who claimed to have investigated these iniquities, and in his report, which was published in a Milwaukee paper, he said that there was "no necessity for state interference."

In a private conversation with Dr. Bushnell, this detective confessed that he never made the tour through northern Wisconsin; never entered but one den, or interviewed but one set of inmates. But his report tended to quiet the public mind, and having in a sense an official stamp would seem to exonerate Governor Rusk. But the terrible facts as witnessed by the brave woman who made a personal investigation of most of the principal cities and towns on all the railroads of northern Wisconsin, proves how misleading were the assertions of the pretended detective. The doctor visited or obtained information of some fifty-nine dens, which were but a part, and of about 575 degraded women: dens of both the ordinary and stockaded kind. The dens are generally situated on the outskirts of the town, in the woods, the dance house proper being the joint product of the saloon and the brothel. The bar room is supplied with piano, violin and girls, in number from ten to thirty, of even fifty. Besides these are managers, bartenders, musicians, watchmen and bulldogs. The girls are hired to dance for their board, receiving one-half the proceeds of their prostitution and half the proceeds of the drinks to which they are treated; but they are required to pay over all the money into the hands of a clerk, who credits one half to the house, the other half to the girl.

The "frequenters" pay twenty-five cents each per dance, and the girls must respond to the call for a dance at any hour of the day or night, and should one refuse to take to her room and man who makes a demand for her, she is fined the share due the house. The girls must be kept in debt, in order that they may be more easily controlled. The whip, the fist, the boot, the revolver and the bull dog are used to keep them in subjection. Broken bones and murder are common, and recruits are a necessity, and agents scour the country in search of poor, pretty and defenseless girls. The busy season of this horrible trade is in the early spring, when the lumbermen from the pineries come into town, when a den made to accommodate a dozen girls will be crowded to hold thirty or fifty, with three or four inmates to a single ten by twelve room. At the town of Merrill the doctor learned of a half dozen girls of a den who were so bruised and mangled that they were a sickening sight.

An inmate of Hunter's den, at Nassau, tells of a sick girl who was dragged down stairs head foremost. But when this den was raided last summer, Hunter lay in jail only three hours, while the victims lay in jail two weeks. A former inmate of Press Wade's den, at Washburn, says he would make the girls go down on their knees and beg, with a loaded revolver at their heads; but when his den was raided the girls were marched through the street in shackles and locked up in cells, while he walked the streets free as any man; and when the den was closed out he simply took his girls over to Ashland, and sold them to another den keeper at $40 apiece. In Ashland a girl was murdered by having her clothes saturated with oil and set on fire. All of these dens are saloons, and most of them are licensed; and the keeper knows that he has his victim as soon as he gets her drucken.

When a girl first arrives her clothes are taken from her and she is obliged to wear the regulation short dress. They generally find as soon as they enter that their traveling expenses are charged against them, the traveling expenses of the procurer and procurer's fee for inducing them to come.

In spite of the showing which den keepers and municipal officers attempt to make that these girls are not detained against their will, the facts remain. As an instance, the doctor visited a lady residing in Hurley, whose veracity was vouched for, who related that last winter between 7 and 8 o'clock in the evening, coming along Second Avenue from town, she heard the clinking of a chain and saw a girl running from the direction of Le Claire's den. Her circular cloak spread out in the wind, her eyes stood out with horror, her dress was caught up at one side, and in her hand was a ball that was fastened around her ankle by the chain which she had heard rattling. She was running as hard as she could and dashed across the railroad just in front of a train; behind her were two men in a cutter. They had to wait a little for the train, and she ran up the embankment and across the Lake Shore railroad, but the men drove rapidly, and overtaking her, thrust her into the sleigh and took her back to Le Claire's den. From one den two escaping girls were captured by the chief of police and brought back: the mistress of the den administering a beating in his presence, the chief making no effort to interfere. Later on one of the girls managed to get out a complaint for assault and battery, but it appears she was mysteriously made away with before the case was prosecuted, and dead women tell no tales.

That these outrages are permitted might be set down to the laxity of the laws of Wisconsin; but we find that they are equal in many respects to those found anywhere in the United States. In Wisconsin a brothel keeper may be arrested on a degree of evidence not considered sufficient by the laws of any other state, and the punishment for procuring or detaining women of previous chaste character is imprisonment in the penitentiary from five to fifteen years. The "age of protection" is 14 years, and penalty for assaulting a woman is imprisonment for life; yet cases are cited of girls under 14 years being kept in these dens, without prosecution against the keepers. In many cases, the officers of the town are men who have kept either dens or saloons in times past, and den keepers who have amassed a fortune can readily influence a certain class of newspapers to whitewash them – their money commands votes, and under the notion that these dance houses improve businesses, merchants and other sometimes aid and abet these keepers.

One who was present at a meeting of the "Business Men's Association," last summer, relates that it was decided to notify a notorious den keeper, who had been driven out of town, that it would be agreeable for him to return, and when his place was rebuilt, printed invitations were to be sent to each business man of the place, with the heading: "Opening of the Summer Sporting Resort." Contagious diseases acts, patterned after those of England, gotten up by the local authorities are enforced in almost every town, the board of health authorizing physicians to make regular examinations of the girls. In one case the mayor of the town was the physician and issued the certificates.

Though few dens were found with the very high stockades that have been reported, yet the system of fines is so rigid, and the shrewd management that keeps the girls almost constantly in debt to the keepers, renders them virtually slaves. Besides, against them is a total lack of sympathy on the part of men and officers, and the determination to maintain these places as a "necessity" and compelling all girls whose appearances are against them to live in these houses, and alas! that it must be said that even some virtuous women demand that their virtue must be protected by the degradation of young girls. A large class of young women have been entrapped into these dens by this tempting offer: "Come north, servant girls are wanted in hotels, and good wages will be paid and no questions asked." Pure girls have been thus caught.

But the law to punish the capture of innocent girls leaves a loophole by which those who can be made to appear as having been previously un-chaste may be enslaved, and guilty men stand by each other in efforts to prove that a girl was "fast" previous to entering the den, and thus they evade the law. These den keepers are almost wholly foreigners, while the inmates are almost wholly American girls.

Do you ask why these atrocities are allowed to go on month after month and year after year? Do you suppose, my sisters, that if in Ashland, Marinette, Washburn, Hurley, and those other towns, the wives and mothers sat in their municipal councils, were represented upon their boards of health, managed all the interests of those towns equally with men, that such a state of affairs could exist three months?

These den keepers have votes, and make and unmake city officers. They are often money kings and carry large amounts of city bonds.

The wives of all these men are helpless – the political slavery of all women, good and bad, makes this vilest of sex-slavery possible. Some atrocities committed are said to be too black for public print, and we know the world's policy has been to keep pure women from the knowledge of these things; yet today all over this land of ours, the spirit of God is moving upon the hearts of women and they are combining their forces and turning a calcium light upon these plague-spots in our midst. Can any woman with the love of Christ in her heart say, "I have all the rights I want," while such slavery of women exists? Suppose we have all the law necessary for the suppression of these dens of vice. It is not enforced. Why? Because too many of the class that makes and enforces law want things to remain as they are.

In a government like ours, a public sentiment must stand behind the enforcement of all law, and public sentiment means here the sentiment of men only; and there are not enough of good men to balance the preponderance of evil men.

While we do not blame men for having come into this legacy of power, yet we believe it has been to them a positive curse. Mark how every step in enlarged opportunities for women has been contested. One of the latest developments of this tendency being the opposition to the appointment of police matrons. The common objection on the part of the officers, say the New York World, is that the women arrested are too depraved to merit consideration, but adds, that the lack of matrons at the police stations is an unnecessary barbarism. Mrs. J.K. Barney, of Rhode island, at the late convention of Christian Workers at Detroit, state that matrons have been appointed in twenty-five or thirty cities, but that every possible impediment is thrown in the way of adopting the system. A few intelligent, virtuous women, jealous of justice to their sex, might prove great stumbling blocks to the machinery of many city governments.

The city of Omaha points with pride to her public schools, which the yearly revenue of $24,000 from her 340 self-confessed prostitutes goes to support.

But what can *we* as an organization do? So world-wide is this vice of prostitution, so world-old is the history of its existence, and so universal is the idea of its necessity, that it seems like attempting to take down a mountain with our toy shovels. One of the saddest facts which meets the man or woman who attempts to work for the suppression of this sex degradation, is the idea which pervades our religion, our literature, our politics, that the woman must be in subjection. That the maternal function is the chief object of her creation, and must be exercised no matter what the result to herself. Even the great reformer, Melanchton (?), says, "If a woman becomes weary of bearing children, that matters not; let her only die from bearing, she is there to do it."

Whether the time be long or short when women shall have political power, in the meantime let us work with such tools as we have, and make our mark upon the age in which we live by a combined effort to make smoother and purer the pathway of our tempted sisters. Shall another year pass and find our own city still without a branch of the "Women's Protective Agency?"

Shall the women and girls who fall into the hands of our police be dealt with only by men? May our continued walk together "make the beaten track appear a little greener where our feet have trod."

Presidential Speech, Iowa Equal Suffrage Association Convention, Ames, IA (December 3, 1891)

(It was not possible to translate this short speech)

Before the WCTU "What has our society done for the franchise" (1892)

Your committee for the program has asked me to answer these questions: What has our society done for the franchise?, What is it doing?, What is it going to do? and Why do we work for the franchise at all?

We will not pretend to answer these questions in the few minutes allowed us, but only make a few casual remarks as we choose.

Twenty two years ago in Dubuque, the state's W. S. Society was born, and from that day on we have been making life unpleasant for our opponents.

But we imagine that we have been the pioneers that blazed the way, cut down the mountains of prejudice, bridged the chasms of ridicule, and helped to make possible the way for the oncoming feet of the sisters of the W.C.T.U. And if we had done nothing else but help to open the way for such a grand organization as this we would feel that our lives had been worth the living. But we have done more; we have been hard at work at the foundation of things, rearing our substructure so what we are doing now is beginning to show above the surface. We have established, and are establishing very many centers of influence throughout the state. Organization is our watchword today. Years ago it was less so.

In our own feebleness we were ready to lean upon the arm of any organization that offered its sympathy; and when your society opened its franchise department, it was hailed with delight; although often when we through our speakers would plant little suffrage societies about the state – along would come the W.C.T.U. and gobble them up. Times have changed somewhat and it is our turn now. But the good seed you have sown, the good seed you are sowing is preparing the harvest by and by. But with your two dozen different lines of state work, when you have made a good W.C.T.U. woman, only one twenty fourth of her is a suffragist.

Naturally with very many women this is not enough and they ally themselves with the society which makes the franchise it's specialty. A certain philosopher says that the test of any principle or creed is the kind in individuals it makes.

We believe that the principles of the W.C.T.U. – We believe that the principles of the perfect equality of the sexes before God and man – help to develop a well balanced character.

We are not rivals, and when you ask what our society is going to do – we answer – We are going to help you – as you are helping us. If you will keep the men sober long enough for them to vote right, we will see to it that power is put into hands of women to help them stay sober.

Lady Henry Somerset said the other day in reply to an invitation to join the Liberal League, of which Mrs. Gladstone is President, that she had for the last seven years given all her time and energy to temperance causes. That churches, politicians, journalists – men of every profession, creed and class were giving active work for it. These efforts have been mainly along the line of moral persuasion, and statistics prove that as yet no marked impression has been made upon the drink habits of England: therefore she had come to demand a machinery that would make the temperance sentiment into law, and women's ballots, as well as brains must help to do it.

One of the wisest mothers in our Israel today says that if the cause of temperance was the one to which she was giving all the efforts of her life, her first work would be to get the vote into the hands of women. Therefore in answer to the question, why do we work for the franchise, we would say it is because it seems to us to be an economy of force. The economic, social and domestic conditions of the average American woman are such that but little time can be given to any work outside the conventional routine. And believing that the duties of the home should not be left undone, our next duty is to work for the larger home-society, and as in our homes we try to make every step count, every effort tells in the largest results to our families, so in the work for the larger home-society, we would put our hands and our limited time upon the lever whose fulcrum is at the foundation of things.

Speech before the Equality Club of Eagle Grove (1893?)

As we read history, we are compelled to seek its gloomiest pages for the record of women. In the long journey of the race from savagery to civilization, woman has moved forward with man carrying a crushing weight of disabilities. We will not now enquire why these things are so, whether they arose from man's love of power, or from his chivalry and desire to protect. Whatever the causes, we here deal only with the fact that woman has been the world's great burden bearer, its great unpaid laborer. Through the ages, this principle has been taught that the subordination of woman was by divine authority.

The creeds of all nations make this the corner stone of her religious character. The most grievous wound ever inflicted upon woman has been this teaching that she was not created equal with man. The world has held that submission to authority and the bearing of children were the two reasons for her being created, and that the woman who failed in either had no excuse for being.

Our missionaries to the heathen find that the degradation of woman is the great obstacle in the way of improvement, for she clings with a zealot's hold to the superstitions of her life, and thus her very religion increases her bondage. For instance among the polygamists of Africa, a native preacher had put away all his wives but one, and this one wife was so unhappy about it that she left him, because, she said, "He looks so mean and poor with but one woman." The same plea of divine authority that created the castes of India and forbids a woman to enter a mosque is the same plea – modified that today forbids women a voice in church councils or state legislatures.

You who have been following the course of study which this Club has recently closed, have observed how through all the events of time and change the idea of individual freedom has been the underlying motive.

The Reformation in the 16th century loosened the grasp of the church upon woman. The American Revolution, its cause based upon the inherent rights of the individual, made a noble background for the final setting forth of the claim for exact freedom for all.

We all know how difficult it is for a new idea to get lodgment in the human brain. Say what we will, there is nothing so costly as an idea.

How long did it take the people of this country to learn what it meant when in the Declaration of Independence it was said that "all men are created equal."

Did it not take one hundred years of travail, the waste of countless treasure, and the slaughter of the first born of every household! As McCauley says, "The highest intellects like the tops of mountains, are the first to catch and reflect the dawn, they are bright while the level below is still in the darkness." So, early in the political history of our country did a few women catch the inspiration of the dawn, and the Declaration of Independence shows the influence of the master minds of those women who bore their part in the Revolution.

Intimately connected with the foremost men of the time were Hannah Lee Corbin and Abigail Smith Adams. Mrs. Adams early protested against the formation of a new government in which women should be unrecognized and was the first American woman who threatened rebellion unless the rights of her sex were regarded. She was the first to counsel separation from the mother country and pressed these views upon John Adams before the opening of the first Congress, when even Washington had no thought of the independence of the Colonies. Our revolutionary mothers certainly did urge the recognition of equal rights when the government was in process of formation.

It is almost impossible to speak of these things without seeming to speak against men. Far be it from me to wish to cast reproach upon the brethren, and I honestly think that the women who believe in equal rights are the best friends that men have in all the world; but in speaking of a system we have to deal with facts the causes of which he perhaps as much in the weakness of women as in the selfishness of men.

Our protest is not against men. Our protest is against the system which men are born into. I could wish no better environment for my sons than that they might go out into the world where every one of God's children has an equal chance. Let us put away from us the idea that this demand of the modern woman for full political freedom is the outburst of a few unbalanced minds. It began out of the political and religious revolution in Germany, France, Italy and America simultaneously by women unknown to each other, this demand for a wider sphere of action in every civilized country.

In this country among the immediate causes was the discussion in several of the state legislatures of the property rights of women, and the able lectures of Frances Wright and Ernestine L. Rose; but more than all was it due to the anti-slavery struggle. The discussion of the great principles of human rights in these conventions taught the advanced men and women of the country how little of the lesson of human rights was yet learned.

Ardent abolitionists of this country and Great Britain, devout clergymen of New England advocated the freedom of the southern black man but could not tolerate the idea of a free woman beside their own hearthstones.

Forty five years ago, the Anti-Slavery Society of Massachusetts placed a woman upon its business committee; later in the same year of 1840, women delegates were elected with men to the World's Anti-Slavery Convention in London. You recall the debate in that Convention of an entire day upon the awful proposition of permitting these half dozen women of America to sit as delegates in this Convention, and that it resulted in their exclusion. But as Lucretia Mott, the charming Quaker preacher, and Elizabeth Cady Stanton, whom we honor today, walked arm in arm away from that Convention to their London lodging; they decided to hold a Woman's Right's Convention on their return to America, and one of that Convention's later children is the promising Club of Eagle Grove, which I have the honor to meet this afternoon. From this small beginning has arisen the vast number of state associations, county societies and local Clubs which spread like a network from the Atlantic to the Pacific and from the Lakes to the Gulf. The women of the churches have found that the spirit of freedom has grown marvelously in the last fifty years.

Judge Tourgee tells of a case in his law practice where an old lady bequeathed in her will her colored man John and his wife Jane to the trustees of a church to be used as far as possible to the "Glory of God." The trustees after deliberation and prayer sold the man and woman at an auction and with the proceeds sent a missionary to China. The church has outgrown this plan of glorifying God.

Our literature has outgrown the thought of Coleridge, that the "perfection of character in woman is to be characterless." With the banishment of this idea, is it any wonder that from the works of the immortal Shakespeare there was much to be expunged before they were fit for the family circle.

What has purified our art? When the art of Greece was in the hands of men only its productions were set in the streets where Greek decorum forbade women to appear, for these works of art were never meant to be judged by women; while later artists like Canova, Flaxman and others never carved marble that may not stand in our parlors for they carved with the ever present thought that mothers, wives and sisters will judge of their work.

Look at our great co-educational institutions today and think of what once was the only means of a higher education for boys, while for girls there were barely the rudiments offered.

In early times in the founding of certain colleges even in this country, provision was made through the funds of the institution, and a room provided where the student young men could indulge their passions, the grave and revered trustees of the institution seeming to regard this as a necessary part of the experience of future husbands and statesmen. Lady Henry Somerset says that "It is characteristic of this age that evil is no longer considered a necessity." Today, 40,000 college girls stand side by side with their brothers on grounds one deemed sacred to men only.

It has been well said that if woman is not to be free it is a fatal mistake to have taught her the alphabet. She has no longer the bliss of ignorance. As women move through history, they discover that almost every custom extant is the gilded remnant of the subordination of our foremothers. The beautiful wedding ring upon the finger of the bride of today is said to be the symbol that the bridegroom's love has no end, but is in fact the remnant of the iron band that bound the wrist of the wife of earlier days.

In feudal times the poor serf man did not own his wife completely. Immediately after marriage for from one to three days the feudal lord had the first right to the new wife, and if during this time the husband ventured too near the castle he was jeered, mocked, and sometimes tortured by his friends. The modern custom of a wedding journey is a reminiscence of that period when the groom and bride would escape the jeers that in earlier ages accompanied the marriage service.

We have grown weary of hearing it asserted that mothers are almost wholly responsible for the morals of their boys; even the good Dr. Parkhurst says "If the mothers of Tammany had been more faithful to their trust, the Tammany of today might not have been." Could anything be more absurd than to demand that mothers shall make the best environment for their children and then shut them out from the privilege of helping to shape that environment? What are our property laws today compared with what they once were?

It is a singular fact of history that the rights of property have everywhere been recognized over the rights of persons. To deny to any individual the right to the proceeds of his own labor is the foremost element of slavery, and when Common Law forbade woman's inheritance and ownership of property, she virtually became the slave of her husband. Her use of any portion of the property without his consent was regarded as theft.

The condition of the unmarried woman was even worse. In 1893, in less than one fifth of the states of this Union has the mother the same control over the children as the father. He can bind them out, will them, or give them away without her consent or even knowledge. We are thankful that our courts are often more merciful than our laws. It is less than 60 years since a change in this respect has taken place in any part of the civilized world, and it is significant that not until women began to ask for the ballot were there any changes in the law favorable to women. It is only when wrongs find a tongue that they become righted. Much has already been accomplished, yet the 20th century opens with the remnants still hanging over us, were it not so, this company would not be gathered here this afternoon.

If it was an outrage for King George to tax the colonists without their consent, it is an outrage for the men of Iowa to tax women without their consent. No man can take the property of another without his consent, neither can a body of men, and every dollar of taxes extracted from the women of this state is so much legalized robbery. We do not object to paying our proportion of taxes, but we do object to the system under which this money is extracted from us.

Just here let us recall an incident of certain modern legislation. A few years ago there was introduced into the Iowa Senate a bill asking that one half of the joint earnings after marriage should belong to the wife. This bill was referred to the Judiciary Committee composed of fifteen members among them the most pronounced advocates of woman suffrage in the Senate. The friends of the bill were very courteously given a hearing before this committee, but when it made its report to the Senate, every man voted against it.

If we accept the story in Genesis that women started the world in the clothing business furnishing the fig leaves for herself and husband, it is pathetic that the evolution of six thousand years does not permit the wife to own her clothes. You probably saw the account in the papers the other day of the man in Connecticut who was so displeased with the fancy gowns which his wife persisted in wearing, that he destroyed them. He was arrested for this destruction of property, but nothing could be done with him, because, as he showed, he had a right to do what he pleased with his own clothes.

We who are suffragists are sometimes taunted by those women who say they have all the rights they want, with the assertion that we are women who want to wear our husband's clothes, while they and the rest of us have always been wearing men's clothes; it is the suffragists who are trying to get women to be allowed to wear their own.

In only a few states of this Union do women yet own the clothes they wear. It took the women of Massachusetts eleven years of hard work before their State Legislature to secure to the wife the legal right to be buried in the family lot of the husband. That our statute books have not yet been cleared of the spirit of the past is evident by the very general demand now being made before the State Legislature for a more definite safeguard for women and girls.

Did not the heart of each one of us leap for joy when the State Federation of Women's Clubs recently in session at Cedar Rapids resolved to ask the next General Assembly for the better protections of our young girls?

We think the country is a great loser by having so long prohibited the financial ability of women from exercise in government affairs. Women's native capacity to make a little money go a great way, and her quick apprehension of details is sadly needed in our municipal affairs especially which are said to be the worst in the world.

By the way, have we not all marveled why in the last few years, there has been such a scarcity of women tramps. Gov. Larrabee once said in a speech, "Did you ever hear of a woman tramp?" Women work from early dawn 'till late at night with no claims for less hours of labor, at one third less wages on an average than men." We admit, that the economic conditions of today are fearfully bad, but while thousands upon thousands of men have been fed by charity, their complement of women has not been asking alms.

A few mornings, since I heard a light rattling of irons and looking up saw upon the street the Des Moines chain-gang marching to its day's walk cleaning the streets.

The questions naturally arose where are the women offenders to match these fourteen stalwart men who are piloted each day by a policeman with his club, to and from city jail?

The same disparity of sex holds good in our two state prisons.

Now the difference in population between men and women in this state, or in Polk County is not enough to account for this difference in number between the sexes. The thought may arise here with some of you why, if women are more industrious and law-abiding, now, under their restrictions, why not keep them there, and reduce a large class of men to the same plane, if it works so well.

This is one feature of the great social and economic questions of the day, and we suggest that they be made the subject for discussion at some meeting of your Equality Club.

We who are asking for the ballot for women are trying to revolutionize by reform, not to reform by revolutionizing. The ballot is the most peaceable and orderly method yet devised for the expression of opinion. It does not govern as the cannon governs. Army and navy, all the brute force of a nation yields before the expression of opinion.

But we need not tread the well worn highway of assertion, we have the proof of a quarter of a century of its actual workings in Wyoming.

From Nebraska to the Pacific in proportions to the number of people, Wyoming has scarcely more than half as many law-breakers as these other states and territories.

These statistics are from the official reports of 1890; then Nevada had one fourth less populations than Wyoming and two and three fourths as many criminals;

Montana; nearly three times as many criminals. Arizona with the same population as Wyoming, had three and one fourth times as many offenders. When these figures were compiled, women in Wyoming had had full political freedom for twenty one years, yet during all this time not one woman had been imprisoned for any offence whatever; and now the latest report after a quarter of a century of women in politics, that state has not a woman criminal.

I believe I saw in the daily paper the other day that there was a woman in jail there, but I presume she just came across from another state where women can't vote.

It is also shown that people stay married there better than in any other state, and one of the first acts of its Legislature after women were given the ballot was to make the pay of its women school teachers the same as for men.

Henry Ward Beecher once said in a speech, "The day in which the intelligent cultivated women of America say, 'We have a right to the ballot' will be the day in which they will have it. The reason you have not voted is because you have not wanted to; because you have not felt it was your duty to vote." But why should we expect the average woman to say that she wants to vote? Ninety nine pulpits out of every hundred have taught that women should not meddle in politics. Almost as large a proportion of the newspapers have done the same; and by the hearthstone, the lesson has been repeated to the little girl, and when she is growing, if she does not throw away the teaching of a lifetime, we blame her for being unprogressive.

Today I think there is no argument used so extensively or is harder to meet than this; the great mass of women do not want the ballot.

There is not positive proof that this is true, but if it were true, there is abundant reason for it, and some excuse. We do not believe the God of justice has left himself without a witness in any age; yet legend and history have been saturated with the principle of woman's subordination. Even our juvenile readers have carried this lesson unmistakably. There is not a bright girl of ten years in all the land but has learned that the world is not all open to her; even in the common things of every day. I have a young daughter, the younger of a family of boys;

healthy, active and strong as any lad of her age, and my heart has asked for over and over, as the hard lesson of a girl's limitations have come to her.

Some years ago the boys had a turning pole set up in the back yard where much fun was had in the art of making muscle. My little girl came to me one day begging, while the tears were close behind the words, "Mamma, I can turn on that pole as good as the boys, and why can't I?" The time has come thanks to the gymnasium and the gymnasium costume when she can spin 'round a pole equal to the best of them.

A wise and learned man has said, "He who has deprived me of my right to vote has done me a great wrong, but he who has deprived me of my wish to vote has done me a greater wrong." But we think that much that is made of the fact of women's indifference to the ballot is pure bravado. We are always a little suspicious when a gentleman makes haste to assure us that he believes in this thing but that his wife is very much opposed to it.

The Iowa Woman Suffrage Association, of which this Club is a component part owns a lovely cottage upon the State Fair Grounds at Des Moines. This cottage has windows upon every side, and here each year do the suffrage women keep open house with petitions to the Legislature for women suffrage, for the signatures of the passers by. Some characteristics of the moving masses at State Fairs during the years have impressed us. When a party of gentlemen and ladies came up if the men sign the petition with a hearty good will and word of cheer, success with the whole party is generally assured; but if the man turns away with a shrug or word of contempt for the measure, it is almost useless to speak to the woman at his side.

Young women with their lovers as well as wives of sixty or seventy shrink from an act that will bring upon them displeasure from ones they love or upon whom they are dependent. We overheard a middle aged woman who had signed the petition say to her grown-up daughter as they turned away, "Katie, don't let father know that I signed this paper."

This timidity is not true of all women, but a long course of observation in this state leads us to believe that there is a vast deal more of woman suffrage sentiment than Iowa men know anything about.

Near twelve years ago our beloved Mrs. Margaret W. Campbell, whose long service for women is known to some of you, made a lecturing tour in the interest of this cause through the northern counties of Iowa. She told me on her return, that sometimes after making an address, some woman in the audience would come to her and with tears in her eyes would say, "Mrs. Campbell, I have had these same thoughts myself but I did not know that anyone else had." We do not know whether a majority of women in this country want the ballot but we do know that a very large and increasing number do. When the ballot was given to the colored man, it was not because he asked for it. The government cared not a fig whether one black man in a thousand wanted it. The objection to woman suffrage lies deeper than the fact that a majority of women have not asked for it.

My sisters: let us stand together and demand that the foundation principles of the government shall be applied to us, one half the people. Organization is the Archimedes screw that moves the world. Self culture is well, but the highest culture comes with the doing the best work of the hour. Let us never cease to be grateful that our lives have been cast in the pleasant places of this nineteenth century era; and the best return we can make for our privileges is to make the most of them. It is said that a learned man is a statue, but a learned man with a task is a living soul. Let us see to it that in these passing days the precious spikenard (?) of life is not spilled in the presence of our glorious opportunities.

"For What Purpose Do We Live?" (ca. 1894)

For what purpose do we live? Are there any prizes in the battle of life worth winning? Or if we fail, is the discipline of the pursuit worthwhile? These questions are absurd upon the face of them, but especially so when given before a company of young men and women. But there is a philosophy which just now sufficiently obtains (?) to merit consideration.

A young man said to me recently that he believed that when a person's life had become a burden and was of no further use to himself or anyone else, and as we are not responsible for having come into the world, that it would be a justifiable act to take himself out of it. Another young man who was then passing through a most bitter disappointment, when the future was all dark to him, said to me, "What matters it whether I am happy or not; I am in the world for a purpose, and I will rise up and do my life work in it." His ideals were higher than the attainment of his own happiness and he was determined to follow his ideals whether joy came to him in their pursuit or not.

After all are not the things which we cannot see or handle the only real things? The things that go to make up the hard wood of character and which stay with us forever? President Garfield well expressed this idea when he said that he wanted to be able always to respect himself, for he was obliged always to live with himself.

You who have been thinking God's thoughts after him along the lives of Evolution have no doubt concluded that it is not likely that the age in which we live happens to be the culminating age; but that the better is always succeeding the best, and that there is a "far off Divine event toward which the whole creation moves." So nothing in nature is without its object – no blade of grass – or drop of water – or pebble upon the shore, must the human production be the one exception?

Surely no one believes but that God has a definite purpose in the life of every one of us. The trouble is not here; but do we have an object in the life that is given to us? Have we ideals? Do we not often as the days go by ask ourselves the question, "What is it all for?" Are we drifting, just moving along in the line of least resistance and expect to keep doing this until the time comes for us to leave it?

I do not believe I am speaking to persons of this class. But is self-cultivation the highest ideal? Is the sharpening of the tools for work of so much importance that the best of our life should be spent in the sharpening and only the minimum left for service? This afternoon of the century demands more of its young men and women than that they be cultured. Prof. Suring said that, "A learned man is a statue, but a learned man with a task is a living soul."

The intelligent people of today have no excuse to be deluded by the gibberish of the astrologer and the alchemist. The sciences have been working themselves, clearer and clearer and depositing impurity after impurity and we do not believe any age has passed certainly not any century but has left some residue of truth. Facts have accumulated, ideals have enlarged and, if the epitome of ten million years is written in the present structure of a minuscule, then we have been born into a splendid heritage; "heirs of all the ages in the foremost files of time." Someone has said, "Every new truth has its birthplace in a manger, lives thirty years and is crucified, and then deified." It is our work to pass on these accumulations to the generations that are to be.

Make the world better is becoming the slogan of today, and our conflict is <u>now</u>, and our field of labor is <u>here</u>. Palestine is holy ground as the birthplace of the world's highest ideals, but our land is the birthplace of our highest thought, and to you young men and women these halls are holy ground. There are a thousand ways in which to make the world better, and we thank heaven for this. There are so many wrongs to be righted, so many different points of view at which to take them that there may be a thousand workers aiming at the same point, but by different routes.

We believe in specialties. The regulation of the affairs of this world has become a system so complicated, there are so many converging lines towards the one point of bettering the condition of humanity that the age of specialties is surely here. We have come to have great patience with the hobby-rider. Indeed we are inclined to be impatient with the person who has no hobby. The man or woman who is today perfectly satisfied with the way the world is getting on and feels that nothing is required of him or her in respect of it, and has no more thought for one plan than another, we doubt if they are worth their salt.

Now you may begin to suspect that I have a hobby. It may be that I speaking to you this morning in spite of the fact that I have a hobby; but I suspect that I am speaking to you because I have a hobby; and this hobby is a soul stirring desire for equal opportunities for all people.

I am no more interested in one sex than the other; the best years of my life have been spent in raising boys whose welfare is more dear to me than my life and if we speak of the wrongs which the world practices towards women it is because these wrongs make life harder for both our boys and our girls; our men as well as our women. It has been well said that if women are not to be free, it was a fatal mistake that they were given the alphabet.

They have no longer the bliss of ignorance. As women move through history, they discover that many of the pleasing customs of modern society are but remnants of the subjection of our foremothers.

The wedding ring upon the finger of the bride of today said to symbolize that the love of the bridegroom has no end is in reality but a beautiful remnant of the iron band that bound the wrist of the bride of long ago. The chivari and wedding journey is a reminiscence of that feudal age when the newly married serf was jeered by his friends because the lord of the manor had prior claims upon the bride.

It is a singular fact of history that the rights of property have everywhere been recognized before the rights of persons. Property is a delicate test of the condition of a nation. The American revolution arose from an attack upon property rights. If it was an outrage for King George to tax the colonists without their consent, even when this tax money was used in protecting the colonies; it is today an outrage for the government to tax the women of this country without their consent. No man can take the property of another without his consent; neither can a body of men. It is less than sixty years since a change in the laws favorable to women has taken place in any part of the United States; and none of these changes occurred until women began to ask for the ballot. Only when wrongs find a tongue do they become righted! Since women have entered the literature, it has outgrown the thoughts of Coleridge that "The perfection of character in women is to be characterless."

What has purified our art? When the art of Greece was in the hands of men only its productions were set in the streets where Greek decorum forbade women to appear, for their works were never meant to be judged by women while later artists never carved marble that may not stand in our parlors.

If we accept the story in Genesis that a woman started the world in the clothing business furnishing the fig leaves for herself and husband, it is pathetic that the civilization of 6000 years does not yet permit a woman to own the clothes she wears. Surely, one fifth of the states of this Union yet allow this. You probably saw the account in the papers awhile ago of the man in Connecticut who was so displeased with the fancy gowns which his wife wore that he destroyed them. He was arrested for the destruction of property, but nothing could be done with him because as he plainly showed he had a right to do what he pleased with his own clothes. We who want to vote are sometimes taunted with the assertion that we want to wear men's clothes, while women have always been wearing men's clothes; the suffragists are trying to get for women the right to wear their own.

We are often asked why if women really have any grievances that more of them do not come out and protest against them. We do not wonder that so many women do not make a public protest against their environment. Ages of repression have had a most benumbing effect upon the undertakings of women. They have learned their lesson of subordination well. Ninety nine pulpits out of every hundred have taught that women should not meddle with politics. Almost as large a percent of the newspapers have done the same; and by the hearthstone the lesson has been repeated to the little girl, and when she is grown if she does not throw away the teachings of a life-time, we ask why she is not progressive.

But the gymnasium and the bicycle are two great – heaven sent – emancipators of women; and girls when you are inspired to do a right thing, and a sensible thing, do not be afraid of Madam Grundy. Even if she should come to you in guise of a good young gentleman; if the mask were torn off you would still see the face of Madam Grundy.

Is there anything in the system of a representative government that is of necessity corrupting? The ballot is the most peaceful and orderly method yet devised for the expression of opinion.

(Author's note: Page 16 is missing of her handwritten copy.)

...them there and reduce men to the same plane if it works so well. This is one feature of the great social and economic questions of the day and we suggest that it be made a subject for discussion at some meeting of our Society.

The suffragists are accused of treading the well worn highway of assertion in support of their claims. Let us see what is proven by a quarter of a century of the actual working woman suffrage in Wyoming. These statistics are from the records of 1890. From Nebraska west to the Pacific in proportion to the population, Wyoming has scarcely more than one half as many criminals as the other states and territories. Nevada has one fourth less population than Wyoming and two and three fourth times as many criminals. Arizona, with the same population and Wyoming has three fourth times as many offenders, Montana three times as many, and now after women have had full suffrage in that state for a quarter of a century, Wyoming has not a woman criminal.

Since writing this paper, we have seen that there is one woman in jail there. We presume she ran across the line from a state where women are not allowed to vote. The records show too that people stay married there better than in other states; that while in the United States divorces have increased 38 percent, in Wyoming they have decreased 29 percent.

One of the first acts of the legislature after the women were freed was to give the women school teachers the same pay as men. In the prison statistics of the other states we find that quite a proportion of the criminals are young men. Now men have been born and raised in Wyoming since women there were absolutely free. We are told that if women are allowed to vote that they will be likely to neglect their children and forget home duties. Then why is it that in 25 years there should be a much smaller number of offenders where women are free than in any other part of the United States?

Suffrage Club: "Men Tramps vs. Women Tramps" (1894?)

We have often wondered why there is such a scarcity of women tramps. If men tramps are a necessary result of the present industrial condition, and if the number of men and women are about the same, why is it that where there are a thousand men asking charity, there are not ten women? The number of occupations open to men are vastly greater, the wages better, the opportunity to go from one place to another greatly in favor of men. We are everlastingly told that men support women. While many of the unemployed are single men and boys, yet the number of that class in proportion is not so large as seriously to affect the calculation. There are single women and girls to match all these. Does anyone imagine that these thousands of idle men are sending home money to support this complement of wives and sisters? If it be true that thousands of men during the last eighteen months would have starved if outside help had not been given, then by parity of reasoning this country should now be dotted from Maine to California with the graves of women who have starved to death. For these women have not asked public charity, but we all know that when money grows scarce, the home is generally the first place to feel the stringency.

During the last winter in all our large cities as in Chicago, the floor of the City Hall was packed at night with sleeping men kept warm by public expense, and a breakfast furnished by charity; how did food and warmth come to the same number of poor women and girls?; for they were not in the City Hall, nor were they on the streets, neither was there a wholesale dying of starvation.

Do we say that the occupations of women have been less affected than those of men?

Ask the scores of clerks, bookkeepers, stenographers and others and see if they will tell you if it has been an easy matter to secure a paying position. Even in domestic employment there has been a sensible falling off. The wages of a domestic with her attendant expense is a heavy demand upon the family purse, and often retrenchment begins just here. It is true the demand for competent help is still large as the advertisement in the daily papers show; but there are thousands of incompetents and those who could not enter domestic service even if places could be made for them. No, the financial problem for women cannot be solved by remanding them all to domestic service; neither does this one open door of employment account for the scarcity of women tramps.

Prof. Drummond says that, "Civilization began when our savage ancestors felt the first spark of human affection, and that the most stupendous work God ever undertook was when he began to make a mother. When the savage mother made the first bed of leaves she laid the foundation of the modern home. The love of the mother for her child came first; all else was a later acquisition."

Possibly, this care for others beside ourselves which Prof. Herron holds is the only true interpretation of the Christ spirit, is yet a little stronger in women than in men. They will stay by the broken fortunes of the family to the very last. In the final analysis it may be found that women have less pride than men; that when the wolf actually looks in at the door they are ready to fight him back with any weapon they can reach. If fair pay is not to be had for their work they will take what they can get, but go on working at something, and live on less and less, but to band together and on a strike is to most women farthest from their thoughts. Women seem not to have imbibed the fatal fallacy that the world owes them a living. We are not holding up to you the actions of women as models of excellence, but this we say, that if men in distress were moved by precisely the same spirit that governs the actions of the women of this country, there would not be droves of idle men meandering through the land asking alms of the thrifty.

I do not say that under our serious economic conditions that strikes and commonweal armies are to be condemned. I only call your attention to the difference with which men and women have met the financial and industrial trouble. We agree with our social economists that we have fallen upon calamitous times; when the rivalry for existence is simply terrible; but in spite of the assertion to the contrary, we insist that history does repeat itself, and that the same causes which worked disaster to primitive civilizations are working towards the same results in the more complicated society of today.

Mr. Benjamin Kidd in his recent book, Social Evolution, shows with remarkable clearness the road by which former great civilizations have travelled to their destiny. That Greece, whether under the rule of an oligarchy, an aristocracy or its independent city states to the "pure democracy" of which our own states have been compared, went down before the canker within her own vitals. The leading principle of Greek society was that consideration was due to the order, but below this human beings were of no account only for plunder. Of the universal brotherhood of man, the Greek mind had no conception. Its civilization shows to us that no sort of a social system can stand the stress of time and change no matter how great its culture if a large proportion of its people are in irremediable subjection.

Roman civilization which exhibited the very highest type of successful military supremacy, repeats the same story -- a high intellectual condition among the ruling classes and a large percent of the population without rights of any kind -- with an almost absurd toleration of all other religions, yet not place for the spirit of the Nazarene who taught the equality of all men. Roman civilization teaches us that in spite of great military prestige and the highest culture, any organization that holds a large class in subjection has in it a poison which, being inseparable from the system, needs time to do its fatal work.

Will our Western civilization prove an exception to this law of development which has worked through all the ages and will work on in-spite of theories and systems? Will our great subject class achieve the goal of equal opportunity without shattering the whole fabric when all former attempts at republics have failed? But what has all this to do with the question of men and women tramps? Much every way. Our country is now in the throes of a terrible industrial depression. And why? Far be it from me to presume to give either the reason or remedy. I come only as one of the great army of the interested with my tribute of wonderment as to why these things are so. With plenty of money in the country and a panicky money market -- with our granaries full and the people asking for bread -- when neither war, famine, nor pestilence has devastated our land, yet apparently no work for thousands of willing hands to do; and strangest of all – with evolutionist, scientist, philanthropist, religionist and hosts of other thinkers racking their brains for the cause and solution, and none able to give it.

This pseudo representative government of ours is but the larger household. What think you of the success of that family where there is a rather good but very busy father, a large flock of children, and no mother? Suppose this father declares before his household and before high heaven that the complicated machinery of his modern home needs another manager than himself, and resents any offers of help as an insult to his high prerogative. Is it any wonder that there is confusion and waste in this household; that though the pantry may be stored yet the children are hungry and chaos and confusion reigns in every department?

If there could be injected into our governmental organization the thrift, tact, economy, and patience in detail that exists with the women of this country – together with that spirit that make a woman self-supporting member of society where a man would turn tramp – then we would have a governmental housekeeping such as the world has no conception of. Then if Christ should come to Chicago or any other city, he would find no political pariahs – no subject class. He would find that the spirit of brotherhood of man which he brought to earth nearly nineteen hundred years ago had come to full flower in our body politic. He would find that the world-old antagonism between the sexes had become a thing of the past.

That our western civilization had come to admit that God knew what he was about when he made men and women different that together they might form the perfect whole; for "sure as sin and suffering joined. We march to fate abreast."

Prof. Herron says that his country is now laboring under "a deep conviction of sin." This gives us hope. It is amazing how slow our American people are to perceive that we are a nation of liars. After fighting to the death for the principle that a free people cannot be governed without their consent and then go to go on for more than a hundred years coolly governing one half the population – taxing them – arresting them – imprisoning them – trying them – hanging them, and permitting them no more voice in the matter than if they were so many South Sea Islanders.

That the masses so far fail to see this gigantic brand we suppose is due to the same thickness of scull that obtained in primitive times when the materials which make our present comfortable homes lay all about our grinning ancestors, yet they kept right on hanging by their tails in the woods. Organized lying has for its sure complement organized stealing. Individual robbery is not uncommon, but our organized robberies cry aloud to heaven.

We are not pointing the way to an economic millennium, but we insist that the working men of this country need in this government the leverage of the ballot in the hands of the working women of the country …a force, the needs, and aspirations of which run side by side with theirs. The capitalist needs the balancing power of woman's vote even more.

We have faith to believe that the expansive capacity of our institutions is so great, and the character of the rank and file of our ruling class is so high, that before it is everlastingly too late, this government which has always acknowledged the fatherhood of God, will come at last to recognize, in its fullness, the brotherhood of man.

Iowa Equal Suffrage Association Convention, Independence, (Nov. 18, 1896)

Mrs. President, members of the Convention and citizens of Independence.

When some of the good people of your city said to the Iowa Woman Suffrage Association, "Come to us with your Convention," then the recording angel wrote it down in his book that the people of Independence were a long way from mound builders. We are glad to have the opportunity to come to your beautiful city. We chanced to read the other day that the dwelling places of the great peoples of the world cluster about a certain parallel that is a golden mean between the too freezing north and the too burning south, and of the five great cities of the world to be north and three be south of a dividing line which runs through the city of

Independence, Iowa. We read also that the instincts of the human race may be trusted, and if we would be in luck, we must live either north or south of this fortunate line.

Now some of us who chance to live considerably south of this line are afraid that we are outside of charmed circle of great peoples, and we are glad that for once we have come up into good society. Your courtesy does not consist in the single fact that you have opened your hearts and homes to your neighbors in Iowa. You have done more than this. You have welcomed to your city the representatives of an idea.

We come to you not as "new women;" indeed, some of us lack a great deal of being <u>new</u>. The idea which we represent is the product of all that has gone before. We represent a class which is hungering and thirsting for freedom. Our pilgrim fathers thought that liberty meant freedom to worship God as they pleased. Their sons saw a deeper meaning in the word for it meant to them that England should not tax them without their consent.

But for the modern woman to talk about liberty may seem to some of you very absurd. Why should women who at home are well housed, and well fed; whose husbands and sons are kind, and considerate; where the men of the households are just as good as the women; why should such woman as these come up here and talk about liberty. We women can't very well help being the descendants of our ancestors. The blood of the patriot fathers flows in our veins too, and every drop of it boils with indignation because we are not free women.

We are now at the door of the 20th Century. Yet, women wear today the heavy restrictive garment that was fashioned for the women of the 18th Century. We are often politely reminded that the women of the U.S. are the most free, and the most fortunate of any women in the world. We believe all this and were are profoundly thankful to every mother's son who helped to make us so. But why shouldn't we have all these privileges. Why shouldn't we be allowed every right that any other human being is allowed?

The day for tears has gone by. Miss Susan B. Anthony said years ago she wished the women would quit crying so much. The W.C.T.U. women are shedding a good many tears yet, but we have done enough of it. We do not propose to "be like a hedge hog rolled up the wrong way, tormenting himself with his prickles." We propose to gladly use the privileges we have to help us to obtain more and there are a thousand different roads through which grists are coming to our mill.

Popular thought is turning our way. Clubs, societies and organizations of women prove that women are learning to combine their forces and stand together. What matters it that they do not all wear our label. They are standing together for something. They are helping to popularize the thought of women's individuality. We imagine there never was an association like ours that had such a large following outside of its actual membership. So we say all hail to the women's clubs, the missionary societies, the Christian Associations, the King's Daughters, and that greatest organization, the Woman's Christian Temperance Union. Let the anti-suffragist lay his ear close to the earth and he will hear the steady tramp of the thousands of oncoming women.

Sir Walter Besant, the English writer, complains seriously that women are invading the employments of men. Now Sir Walter Besant and all the rest of them were contented enough until women began to enter the professions and to take salaried positions; and this financial independence of women has worked a wondrous change. There is an army of bright working girls who pass my door each morning with elastic step and heads erect, whose whole bearing says plainly, "I am earning my own living, thank you."

But women have dragged down the wages of men; and great is the pity of it. They have quietly slipped into the poorly paid places. They have preferred this to marching across the country in droves like Kelly's army. This is the natural outcome of our strained economic relations. We are confronted with a condition the causes for which lie deeper than gold, silver or the tariff. We realize too that it is better to fight for the good than to rail at the ill; but we do protest against that system of government which enfranchises the saloon and the gambling house, and disfranchises one half of the home and two thirds of the church.

We Iowa people are not doing as we might, though we imagine we are in the forefront of progress. In my own city of Des Moines where we think very highly of ourselves, we have saloons – and a white chapel district. We have a chain gang and our courts have sent 37 men to the penitentiary within a year – and we will soon have the Legislature. Now it takes all the good people of a city to take care of all the vice of a city, or it is not taken care of. We are working upon a scale of uneven balances. Our political dreamers have again and again come to their several fig trees, but the time of figs was not yet. A government must be just or it cannot be saved.

So the Woman Suffrage Association comes to sharing its vision of justice _____ that you in the breadth of your sympathy have welcomed the humble advocates of absolute justice in government has made the Iowa Woman Suffrage Association your gracious debtors.

Again, we thank you.

Iowa Equal Suffrage Association Convention, Boone, (October 6, 1903)

(Author's note: The copy is somewhat difficult to read and is subject to transmission errors.)

Why are we assembled here today? It has been at some inconvenience, some sacrifice. Have we found that our environment in the world is not the best for our development. That the work which needs our doing is hindered because of the environment. Believing that neither man nor woman can do their best work under present conditions; then being people of good sense, we the people here assembled from all parts of the state do solemnly declare that we will change these conditions.

We believe we are right. We believe our cause has the sanctions of the great head of the church; with whom there is neither Jew nor Greek, bond or free, male or female, for all are one if we are Christ-like. For the present condition of women in this country, history furnishes no parallel. In the days of savagery, women were bought or stolen. They were useful to work and bear young and thus were necessary to their clan. In Homeric Greece, nomadic Judea and the old Germanic ages, men had come to see that women could be utilized in the industries and in a great emergency might fight, or even govern. Through convent life of the Middle Ages, the Italian Renaissance and through the later chivalry of even the 18th Century, woman was still a plaything and parasite.

In the 19th Century, women entered upon a new role. Men, in working out freedom for themselves had become broad enough to see glimmerings of the rights of the individual. But how hard it has been to learn that even <u>men</u> are all created equal --- the tens of thousands of graves all over our southland show. To take the scales for our blind eyes to see that this country could not hold together half slave and half free, the destroying angel had to stand for four terrible years spreading his black wings over every household. Today, white women and black stand side by side in privileges and restrictions in a relation in which the two race classes never stood before.

Last year, 1,000,000 immigrants came to this country to better their condition. The larger portion of these were from the lower classes of the east and southern Europe. They are settling very largely in our cities to grow discontented whenever wages are lost. We welcome the honest homemakers from all lands. But even an ignorant anarchist may come to our shores and in a few months after landing may vote the conditions under which the women of that state must live. Why should not the slum element of all Europe come here? They not only become free from despotism themselves, but they become the political masters of the women of this newer country. I do not believe that good kind hearted men could look their wives and daughters in the face if they realized the enormity of this injustice.

At the opening of the 19th Century, no government money was expended in the education of women and girls. Today, there are 77,000 more girls than boys in our high schools. The whole system of primary education is in the hands of women and the higher education is threatened with the same result. These teachers are expected to imbue the minds of their pupils with patriotism, and a love for the government. This government that says to every high school girl that no matter how good or how learned she may become, her opinion will be of no account at the ballot box where her environment is decided. History has no precedent for an absurdity like this. Again we have the political absurdity of members of a class being elected to an office for which they are held to be incompetent to vote. All over Iowa on the second Tuesday of next month will be an election for the Iowa Superintendent of Schools – yet at not a ballot box in the state will she be allowed to vote.

In the church, two thirds of the membership are women, and they long ago took the burden of church work upon themselves. The Methodist Church, perhaps the greatest leader in morals in this country during the last two centuries, opens its theological schools to women where they may fit themselves for the ministry; then refuses to ordain them to preach. A majority of Episcopal churches still do not permit their women to vote even for what men shall fill the office of vestry men. In the great Christian Endeavor Society, which claims over 4,000,000 members, women form two thirds of the mighty host, but they have no official voice in the administration of its affairs.

We hear today of the alarm about "race suicide," that our women are less willing to become mothers. If this be true, is there not a crying cause in that this government refuses to protect the offspring of women. It is a hard thing to say but it is true that this government of men only is in the business of destroying the offspring of women. This government virtually says to women, go help make homes, bear children and every year we will lay 100,000 of them in drunkard graves besides those whom we will put in our alms houses, penitentiaries and insane asylums. Do you wonder that a woman will go out upon a ranch and go to raising sheep instead of boys and girls. She knows that if wolves attack her sheep that the government will step in and offer a bounty for every wolf's scalp. When men make the raising of children as safe as the raising of sheep and calves, then will our daughters cheerfully become wives and willing mothers.

But say what we will about the great reform yet to be accomplished, nevertheless, we are proud over the present condition of American women. School, church, society, and in a less degree law have made this that, and the other concessions until the status of women today bears little resemblance to that of a century ago. Then, when the mass of women were ignorant and subjugated and had nothing whatever which they could call their own --- they held themselves at much the same value at which men held them and felt less keenly the humiliation of their environment.

Today, intelligent, cultivated, traveled, in many cases wealthy, their inferior positions in the state compels them to wear a yoke, galling and peculiar, such as no class of intelligent women ever wore since government began.

We are thankful to the men of this country for every concession they have made. We are not here to condemn our fathers, husbands and brothers. This legacy of power over the destinies of women has been bequeathed to them from the generations gone before. They are not to blame for this heritage of power. We wonder indeed that they are as good as they are.

But here in Iowa, we are sometimes confronted with this pertinent question. We boast that it is almost every line of the world's work men have made great advances. Why is it that politically she has been almost at a standstill?

We announce that it is simply and solely because the ballot is a threat – the consent of the whole body of men. In all other directions in the industries, arts and professions, some woman has been brave enough; and there was either the kindness or because he could get her service for less price and __ __ end of the wedge was introduced. Gradually, other women and other employers met on the same terms and thus the industries and professions were opened to women. It needed but a few men and even one man to allow a woman a place. Had it been necessary to ask the whole mass of men whether women should go to college, we would today probably have no more co-educational institutions in this country than we have states granting full woman suffrage. But to get women the ballot, we must have the consent of the whole mass of men.

The founders made this a male government and vested in men the absolute power to prevent women forever from having any share in it beyond paying taxes for its support. This then is the environment which, in our endeavor to change, we have met here today. The powers of our national and state constitutions have mapped out the road by which we and all other classes must travel if we hope to reach the high standards of voters. It seemed utterly impossible to get through legislative enactment, therefore the privilege must either come through an amendment to the national Constitution or by a state Constitutional Amendment which, in Iowa, must run the gauntlet of the votes of 150 men in our State Legislature, and this for two successive sessions, and afterward receive a majority vote of the men of the state.

For thirty two years, by bills and petitions, we have begged these 150 men to submit these question to the voters. From 1871 (?) to 1884, they played see-saw with it: one session passing it and the next one killing it. But since 1884, the continued gain in public sentiment has been so obvious; our Association has so widened its influence and clubs have sprung up in many quarters of the state. The Legislature has determined that the risk shall not be run that this measure might carry at the polls.

But a cause that is worth fighting for is worth suffering defeat for. We know that we have a vast amount of sentiment in our favor. Our work through all those years has not been without results. Our foundation is permanently laid in the hearts of the people. To get our bill passed by the Legislature next winter is the Mecca towards which we now turn. We have three months in which to work. We are here to plan, to counsel and to learn from one another. Let us set every wheel in our machinery to a quickened whirl.

Let us not be beguiled with the delusion that petitions do no good. There are some present here today who could point us to high places in this state where the votes of certain members in the Legislature have been saved to us through the force of the petitions which you delegates have sent up. Let us not grow weary in the work. It is said that even God cannot use a discouraged person. Why should we be discouraged? It has taken men 700 years to bring men's suffrage to its present proportions; while women have not worked 100 years; and today there are over a million fully enfranchised women.

Look at the length of time required to get on the Board of Control. As far back as 1876 Gov. Carpenter suggested a change in the trustee system of managing state institutions. Four years later Gov. Gear recommended a Board of Control. Ten years later Gov. Hull made it a special feature of his message of 1890. Bills were introduced in the legislature on this subject in 1896, 88, 90, 92, 94-96-98 and not until _____ was the law enacted. It took over 20 years to get this much needed change in the management of the state institutions.

We have worked _____ _____longer in an effort to bring about the most radical change ever proposed in the commonwealth of Iowa.

The machinery of our Association is in good working order. Faithfully, women have labored hard the past year to bring the press of the state into line with our thoughts, with what success their reports will show. The letter writers, the workers before large assembles have turned the people to think of our cause. The Headquarters work will show for itself, under the care of our efficient Corresponding Secretary. The field worker will come up bringing their shares with them.

We are here to gather fresh inspiration, look into each other's faces and feel the glow of courage ship in the work of a holy cause. If we are worthy to be the sons and daughters, we must do something for others every day of our lives.

Remember, that "the fault is not in our stars, but in ourselves, if we are underlings."

Iowa Equal Suffrage Association Convention, Panora (November 9, 1905)

There is a great problem confronting the women of Iowa today. The same kind of a problem that has given unrest to men and women ever since governments began. It is this: How to obtain political freedom.

The Declaration of Independence is slowly and painfully being interpreted alright. It required 100 years and the blood of a nation to teach us that all men were created equal. Is it a wonder that it has taken even longer to convince us that all men and women were created equal. It is said that the framers of our National Constitution built better than they knew. Yes, and they built worse. In their recent escape from kingly rule themselves, in their overpowering zeal to vest all authority in the sovereign men people – like all before them they ignored the fact that women were people and vested all power in the sovereign men. Europe has no monarchy within her borders where there is such arbitrary discrimination against women.

The U.S. alone of all countries having an elected representative government cannot or will not extend the franchise to any class without a change in the National Constitution; and every State Constitution requires the same. The English Parliament has absolute power to free its women. Australia enfranchised its 850,000 women. The Parliament of New Zealand by one act freed 150,000 women. Now we have no idea that the forefathers realized how hard they were making the path which their daughters and granddaughters would have to travel in order to reach the political level of themselves.

After the adoption of the National Constitution for about 60 years, women were apparently contented to be silent partners in this compact. But in 1848, a New Declaration of Rights was put forth, signed by 68 brave women who claimed that they too were a part of the body politic, taxed without representation and governed without their consent. From that time on there has been a growing appreciation of human equality as expressed in terms of government. The forgotten one half of the people are yearly -- yes – daily discovering themselves more and more. This growth is from within. <u>Women are finding to their distress and dismay that the legal clothing with which the men of the 18th Century invested them are too small for their expanding bodies;</u> and worse than this, we find that fret and chafe as we may in these outgrown garments, we cannot cast them off until men, the makers of these garments, see fit to remove them.

<u>It is bad enough to be compelled to be governed by living men, but to be governed everlastingly by men who for more than a century have been in their graves is more than women of the present day are willing to stand. As Col. Ingersoll used to say, "When a man's dead, let him keep still."</u> It is not that men are by nature unkind to women. But it requires a fine order of intellect to see an evil that lies about us on every side; and men will evade or resort to expedients for a long time rather than openly attack an established wrong. A blind contentment with the old order of things when we know they are wrong; even though we are not responsible for their being is the beginning of moral death.

Our strengths come from the things we try to do. It is the work of suffragists to stir up our uninterested sisters, our half-awakened brothers. Does this time seem long? <u>It has taken this country 40 years to get the east and west united so that Congress could pass an irrigation law to transform our arid lands; and in this there was neither race nor sex prejudice to combat. For only about 60 years have women been asking for a measure a thousand times more revolutionary than laws for irrigation.</u> No new thing has happened that woman suffrage has not come sooner.

<u>We</u> have a world-old prejudice to combat. The fathers and grandfathers and great grandfathers taught that woman's place was that of a political underling. They early had the divine inspirations for freedom for themselves from British rule, and they fought for it. Do we expect to be "wafted to the skies on flowery beds of ease," while we are working out <u>our</u> freedom? Do we <u>deserve</u> freedom if we will not work for it?

Were I an orthodox preacher, I would probably say that we women should be willing to take up the cross of Christ, and this is exactly what I mean. If our idea of a representative government – our patriotism be secured at; what does it matter? It is worth the need. But the day of need is passing – men are not alone in being held by prejudice. In Eastern countries where women are shut up in _____ and dare not appear in public without their veils, the women themselves are the strongest supporters of these restrictions, for it has been taught them that it adds to their dignity. <u>It is said that when a Hindu gentleman proposes to educate his young daughter that the women of the family threaten to drown themselves. The anti-suffragists of today do not propose to drown themselves to keep women out of politics;</u> they had rather get into politics themselves by making speeches from the rostrums or securing such men as Dr. Lyman Abbott to go before state legislatures and beg them <u>not</u> to give women their freedom.

It is very often said in these days that suffrage is not a natural right. Women have no natural right to ride in street cars. But if women were forbidden to ride in the street cars, would it be very convincing and satisfactory to be told that to ride in street cars was not a natural right? But what would we think of a class of women who would be contented decade after decade to trudge through the streets on foot because society said that it was unwomanly for women to ride in street cars? Yet to refuse women the ballot on the ground that it is not a natural right is not one whit more absurd or unjust and for thinking woman to be utterly indifferent to the present condition in this government is equally absurd.

Again is dust thrown in our eyes by telling us that the family is the political unit. The bachelor who has no one depending upon him has a vote. The widow with six grown daughters has not a vote. Where is the family unit? Suffragists must not be duped with a fallacy like this.

The entrance of women into the labor market has made it imperative that government recognize motherhood as a service to the <u>state,</u> for which the state must be ready to give due protection. Women must be allowed to control the environment into which they are asked to bring fresh human beings. Mothers ought not to live like frightened deer trying to hide their fawn from beasts of prey. It is not fair to mothers that our streets are lined with open doors to drink, degradation and ruin. It is our business, it should be our religion to secure that environment which will produce the highest type of human life here on earth. Let us bear in mind that the prairies of Iowa are as near to the heart of the loving God as were the plains of Palestine when the world was young.

It is claimed that American women are queens. Then it is the business of queens to be queenly, and when a chance comes to do a queenly act, great or small, do, simply and without preparation. How many lovely women do we meet who say, "I believe in woman suffrage; I know we cannot do the best work in the world as things are – but when my children are older, or when this or that is accomplished in my life – then I too will help the cause for which you are working?" In the meantime, the little service – a subscription to a paper or a fifty cent membership in a suffrage club is not given and the cause that would help to uplift humanity is left the poorer by so much. Women who enjoy rights of personal property and of opportunity won for them by the struggles of women in the last fifty years – yet who serenely tell us they have all the rights they want. <u>With the New Testament in our hands, we cannot be satisfied with the present condition of things.</u> We serve God by serving one another. If women fail to do their part, men cannot do it for them and thus are prevented from doing their own work well.

To be harmless after the fashion of women is not enough. Nations in which the masculine virtues only have found expression have gone down; so will our own nation if our women use not their virtues for its safety, and if we are to have a life everlasting, it must have its start here and now. Wherever we are, there is our past of service.

Let suffragists be not unfriendly to the various other causes which are at work for the uplift of the human race – the Church, Temperance, child labor – Direct Legislation and the scores of philanthropies which press upon us from every side. But underlying all these, if it signifies anything to be moral – if it signifies anything to be intelligent – to be a <u>good</u> human being, then in a government like ours, this intelligence, this goodness must have power to put its hand upon our laws. We believe the suffrage work lies not at the center but at the very <u>bottom</u> of reform measures.

What would we think of the farmer who was in earnest to raise a good crop of corn upon his promising acres but who was content to turn the soil with an old fashioned plow with a wooden mould board drawn by a yoke of oxen when a steam plow running a dozen furrows was obtainable but he would take no pains to secure it because the wooden plow and yoke of oxen had been left to him by his father? Women are cultivating what is of more value than corn or wheat. They are raising boys and girls, and need to be able to put the mother heart into the laws. Man suffrage to achieve its present proportions was over 600 years in the making. Are we women so weak of purpose that we are ready to fall by the way because our efforts have not met with success here in Iowa in the 35 years we have been asking for it?

My dear comrades, there was never a time in all these years when our cause occupied such an advantageous position as it does today. Never a time when we knew so precisely where to concentrate our work. The members of the last legislature, with a half a dozen exceptions, and whose views upon our question we learned at that time, are the <u>same</u> men who will return to our legislative halls this winter. Let us between now and January 1 lose not one day of precious time; but put our most intelligent plans and every ounce of energy <u>where</u> what we do will count. Let each one of us go home to our respective counties and be not satisfied though our Senators and Representatives may pleasantly tell us that they rather <u>think</u> they will vote to submit our question; but bolster them up with a special petition with the names of the best voters in their respective counties.

Men always want an excuse for doing wrong, but many legislators want an excuse for doing right. A wise ex-member of the Legislature writes us, "Be sure that you know the sentiments upon the question of every man in the Legislature before he comes to Des Moines." Of the 99 counties of the state, in 24 both Senators and Representatives are believed to favor the passage of the Woman Suffrage Amendment. In 26 counties both Senators and Representatives are supposed to oppose it. The remaining 49 counties are half and half.

My dear friends, we have had a long pull together in this work. In the next three months, let us make a short and a <u>strong</u> pull together in this one and only way – as it seems to me will be effective; and this <u>we can do</u> – and we must or the next legislature may go by as a dozen have gone before. A little time from many of us, and a little money from all of us if <u>well directed</u> will bring the grand result for which we are aiming.

"Political Advancement of Women," Norwalk (1905)

I cannot be told when the first idea of woman's equality had place in the world – certainly as long ago as the days of Plato, 300 years before Christ. All down the centuries here and there have been individuals who believed in equality between men and women. In Colonial days, Margaret Brent asked that she might vote in her state of Maryland. After the French Revolution, more than 100 years ago, _____ asked that female suffrage might be included in the law of the New Republic. But not until 1848 did an organized movement begin when Elizabeth Cady Stanton, Lucretia Mott and others called a convention in Seneca Falls, NY. Here 64 brave women declared themselves for the political rights of women. The years went on and their numbers increased in spite of the storm of opposition which raged around them.

Then came the Civil War when the energies of these women were sought for in other channels. Men high in the councils of the nations said to them, "This is the negro's hour. Cease working for yourselves and help us!!" And they bravely laid by their work for themselves, and circulated petitions to Congress for the freedom of the black man. The war being over, the slaves freed, and the ballot given to all black men. The women of the country again took up the struggle eagerly for their own political freedom.

The Temperance Reform Movement under the leadership of the queenly Alice (?) Francis Willard spread almost like wildfire over the land enlisting the interests of thousands of women. Again were the suffrage women appended to their chosen work. It was told them that, "This is the drunkard's hour." But our women had grown wise. They knew earlier than the temperance women, the serious handicap under which all women labored without the ballot. A dear aged-wise woman suffragist said to me years ago, "Did I care more for the cause of temperance than anything else in the world – to bring success to that cause? I should first seek the ballot for women."

So side by side through these later years has the W.C.T.U. through its department of franchise worked in harmony with the Equal Suffrage Association, and is doing precisely the same kind of work. What have been the gains in political freedom in the last 57 years since 1848? Almost simultaneous with the organized movement in this country did it begin across the water. Australia heads the list in giving political freedom to its women. In Italy, France, Austria – even in Russia have women minor political privileges. England, Scotland and Ireland have given women municipal and county suffrage.

Sweden and Norway are quite advanced – the Norwegian girl who comes over here and enters our kitchen as a domestic; is obliged to lay down some of her political rights, and to sink to the level of her disenfranchised American mistress.

But shameful as it is that even our gallant Iowa men have allowed their far off Norwegian brothers to outstrip them in granting justice to women – still in the Women's Suffrage since 1848 there has been a glorious advancement in securing political privileges. In Wyoming, Colorado, Utah and Idaho, women have the ballot upon the same terms as men. In 22 other states, women enjoy some form of suffrage. In Iowa, women may vote upon municipal bonds, and we expect to vote upon all measures in the not distant future.

In my humble view, never in the last 20 years has the outlook been so favorable as it is in this very month of grace. We believe we have good reasons for being hopeful over the prospect. Since it cannot come too soon, there is an aggregation of wrongs that need to be righted.

Think of all our churches being practically disfranchised. Two thirds of the church membership are helpless at the polls. The churches are seriously charged with not voting as they pray. Surely two thirds of the church do not vote as they pray – devout as they may be. My Sisters – with the New Testament in our hands, how can we be satisfied with this state of things.

We have tried to show a little of the advance towards liberty that women have made. The privileges that are ours today have been won for us. Let us be faithful in our trust.

In regard to child labor in Iowa, it is said with truth that the saloon demands one in every five of our boys for its support – but the increasing demand for wage earning children also demands one in five, and of this number one in every three is a girl.

Iowa Equal Suffrage Association Convention, Ida Grove (Sept. 25, 1906)

I believe I voice the thought of the delegates to this convention when I say we are glad to be here; we were glad to be invited to this goodly place. Years ago, this Association was wise enough to discover that your little city had some of the best and brightest women in the state; and so made one of them our President; and we knew that we had honored ourselves in the doing. Your local club has made our reception so cordial that we are in the finest humor imaginable. Some of us who have come up here out of the dust and coal smoke of a place like Des Moines feel that we have come into an atmosphere so pure which it is almost heavenly; and were it not for the force of habit, we might not be reminded that it will be necessary to wash our hands and faces at all.

But pure air has made pure blood which has flown to the higher arches of the brain and made you thinkers. Emerson says that thinking is the hardest task in the world and there are whole communities preferring not to trouble themselves with the understanding; and like the man centuries ago are wailing still at the pool of Silaam (?). Not so Ida Grove, or it would not have invited the Equal Suffrage Association.

Another of the hard things for human nature to accept is that in this inequality of the sexes (which our mission is to remove), there are none too brave for it. The cause of woman suffrage is not a protest against men. It is a protest against the system in a representative government which falls below the representative ideal. The revolutionary fathers had their ideals of justice and they lived up to them. One hundred and thirty years have passed. The world's ideals are higher today, and if we are even as wise as our great-grandparents in their day, we must be a great deal wiser than they were.

What would you think of a class of people who would be content with the political environment which was mapped out for them a century and a quarter ago by men who had only just caught the idea of political freedom for themselves?

There are thousands of women in Iowa tonight who cannot rest in a contentment which they feel is shameful. So we are trying our best to find God's way out of the wilderness into the Promised Land, and our road seems to be the way of the State Constitution. The framers of our State Constitution – wrapped the precious ballot up so tightly that it takes the action of two sessions of the Legislature, and then a majority vote of the men to break in to the enclosure. We believe that no question has ever come before our State Legislature since the Legislature was created that has had so many petitioners as has the question of giving the voters a chance to say whether or not women shall have the ballot. We believe that if all the petitions upon all other subjects through all the years were lumped together, they would not equal ours in number.

Just here is a curious fact. We have watched this business closely for 35 years, and up to the last two sessions, it has seemed to take the average man (we mean the average legislator) about ten years to get the idea into his head clearly that the suffragettes do not ask them to give the ballot to women. They are asked only to submit the question to the voters to decide. The suffragettes are willing that the fathers, husbands, brothers and sons should decide this question. But we are far from willing that 150 men in the Legislature, or 158 men as it will be hereafter -- vested with brief authority, shall forever decide this question for all the rest of the men in the state.

It is a long cry and far cry from Magna Charta in the 18th Century to the men of Iowa in 1906 that the people have rights which Kings in England and legislators in Iowa are bound to respect. The best system of relegated power may be abused and the rights trampled upon. We believe quite as many men as women have been among the hundreds of thousands of petitioners, and after 35 years of asking, men too are growing tired of the prolonged insult. Men are coming to see that the wishes of wives and mothers cannot be ignored by the legislature without contempt and continually coming upon <u>themselves</u>.

Men are awakening to the fact that an aristocracy of power may grow up even under a representative government. No man is fit for a seat in the legislature who – under conditions like this – is too cowardly or too mean, to trust the people; women are classed sometimes, or perhaps justly, for their forever apparent lack of interest in present Iowa politics. But after all, is it any wonder?

While one great party is eliciting for a progressive or a stand fast leader, and another great party is raking the stubble for votes for a young man upon a composite platform, and both parties are chasing that great American Chameleon, the tariff which turns any color to the party which one takes it in all the political hodge podge of interests where one half of the people are forgotten. We, Iowa women, first of all, and above all things else, desire our political freedom.

So it is our love of freedom that has brought us here tonight, and it was through your love of freedom, through your large ideas of justice, and your gracious kindness of heart that you have invited us.

"In the Service of the King" (Undated)

In the olden times when a royal monarch would make a journey through his primitive domains, it took a large force of his subjects to prepare the way for the passage of the royal cortege. There were no highways to travel; prepared for him, some were sent far ahead into the primeval forests to blaze the way – to chop down the trees, cut down the hilltops and drain the marshes. Another detachment behind them carried away the stones and brush – another detachment made smooth the way with spade and shovel, and yet others worked close to the chariot wheels.

It was a great honor to be called thus into the king's service, especially for those who worked so near the king that all the world could see that they were preparing his way. But to the little hands sent far away over the mountains, out of sight of chariot or sound of bugle – to these the stupid populace who saw not their purpose, cried to them, "What do you here? You spoil our forests – you frighten our game – you make a great noise, only to call attention to yourselves. But they answered while the chips flew, "We make way for the coming of the King."

So friends, in the great onward march of the cause of truth and justice in the world, there are many battalions preparing the way; and it may be that it is the Suffrage Army that is sent ahead to hew down the heavy growths of prejudice, and level the hills of conservatism, and though the slime of the marshes may be upon their garments, yet do they not make more solid the ground and smother the way for the daintier feet of our Club women!

The great army of Temperance workers, the Missionary workers, the Church workers with their place so near the chariot wheels -- all this grand army which is marching tandem through the world – all these -- are in the service of the King.

"Is Philanthropy a Science or a Fad" (Undated)

Your committee for the program has given to me what seems an undebatable question, "Is Philanthropy a science or a fad?" What is Philanthropy? It is a readiness to love and do good to others. What is a fad? It is a trifling pursuit. Now, is a readiness to love and do good to others a trifling pursuit? It is doubtless owing to the failure of many who would bless their kind to properly present the truths they possess that the idea has obtained that Philanthropy is a fad.

But has it become so fashionable to do good that we have begun to counterfeit it? If this be true, then society has taken a long step towards popularizing the Sermon on the Mount. But we apprehend that greed masquerading under the guise of Philanthropy has done much to bring the name into disrepute; the experiment at Pullman serves to illustrate this fact. But that true Philanthropy can be a trifling pursuit argues a degree of misapprehension of which we cannot suspect Unity Club; for of all clubs with which we are acquainted, then would it have least reason to exist. Would anyone presume to say that the application of the Golden Rule is a fad?

But has Philanthropy yet become a science? We believe it is working towards it. Of all the organizations formed to benefit mankind, all, or none, may have the "scientific spirit," which means open to truth on every side, but they have certainly been open to the one truth that our neighbor needs help.

In the world of science, men have their specialties: Fulton in the application of steam; Morse in telegraphy; Edison in electricity, etc., but it is all science. In our present state of development, it seems necessary for Philanthropy to follow the same law. Those who are in earnest must, as it appears to us, concentrate upon their specialty. To get the full force of the current of a river, we must narrow the channel. This may not be our ideal theory of Philanthropy but so far the world seems to demand just this kind of work.

Miss Ida Wells, the brilliant young colored woman who recently visited our city is a fine specimen of Philanthropy concentrated. She has little time to see, hear or sympathize with any other phase of the world's wrongs save those of southern black men – and we are proud of the modern Joan of Arc. A remarkable illustration of this idea is the life work of Rev. D.L. Moody. Prof. Drummond says no other man has done so much directly in the way of uniting man to God, and man with man. In England, Scotland and Ireland, churches, halls and institutions have sprung up in his track. The two great schools at Northfield, Massachusetts and the Bible Institute in Chicago are but a part of his work here; but, says Prof. Drummond, "No other man has kept himself so aloof from fads, isms or special reforms, or from attacking specific sins." Narrow, Rev. Moody certainly is, and perhaps no other man so tries the patience of reformers; but his work is great in results. That he does not attack specific sins is not evidence that specific sins should not be attacked. Quite another man is Dr. Parkhurst, who looks at truth from another side and brings his powerful batteries to pray upon specific sins.

The fiery William Lloyd Garrison, stirring the benumbed spirit of the North to the horrors of slavery; Miss Willard, leading her hosts against the rum power; Miss Anthony and her battalions urging the political freedom of women; these with the specialists in science are among the great forces which are bringing the moral and material world up to a higher level. So let us be patient with the specialists. We are weary of hearing it said, "I do not like such and such people. They are so 'one idead.'" Over and over have we been driven to the conclusion that it is better to have even one idea worth living for, than not to have any. Perhaps you are thinking that, "The party that I belong to is the party that I'm singing this song to: but no man lives unto himself," and "He who puts any part of God's machinery in gear for mankind has the Almighty to turn the wheel."

One of the most hopeful signs of present day efforts and to which the wholesale political corruption should not blind our eyes is the tendency to make Philanthropy practical in the business life of the world. In England where success in municipal government is much greater than in this country, we notice in the city of Manchester where 6,000 persons are in the employ of the city, that the frequency of men dying and leaving their families in want has led the City Corporation to ask Parliament to enact a law by which it is compulsory for employees of the city to take out an insurance policy. Now all the employees receiving not less than $7.50 per week are required to contribute 3.75 percent of their wages; the Corporation contributing the balance. On reaching the age of 65, or becoming incapacitated, the holder is entitled to receive the amount invested plus 4 percent compound interest. In the event of death, it goes, of course, to his family.

In Vienna, the experiment of Josef Hahns (?) with "Peoples Kitchens" where 20,000 people are fed every day, and where a dinner for school children may be had for two cents apiece has proved a commercial success. Think how the great soul of Gen. Booth has wrestled with the problem of how to convert Philanthropy into a science.

Unity Club has undertaken the high mission of bringing into the practical working of a church Club the liberal spirit which the church stands for. We who base our faith upon the order of naïve rather than upon its miraculous disturbance, stand for the task of keeping ourselves open to truth on every side, which is the only scientific spirit, and are in readiness to love and help one another, which is Philanthropy.

It is said the followers of Mohammed are the only enthusiasts who have united the spirit of toleration with zeal for making proselytes. Let us not mistake or fall short of our high endeavor. Sisterly forbearance, combined with sisterly helpfulness, is a double cord to bind us together. It is said to be difficult to help those upon our own plane from lack of vantage ground. Well, the old accepted lines of helpfulness may not be ours to follow. We may not need to lift each other up or lead each other's thought. Possibly, the sweetest service my friend can render me is simply to walk firmly by my side, she thinking her thoughts, I thinking mine, but with our faces set always towards the delectable mountains.

Henry Ward Beecher said, "It has been the rule of my life to work with any man of good morals, on all lines in which we agree, though in a hundred others, we disagree. I work with any man whose face is as if he would go to Jerusalem." There is no time for idling; for if "an angel's wing would droop if long at rest," much more would Unity Club degenerate, for we are not angels. In a world where so many wrongs are to be righted, we dare not spend all our days even in selfculture, for if we wait for all equipment, our ships may have passed in the night.

He who stood before a block of marble and saw an angel imprisoned therein and with faithful hand set it free, we call a great sculptor: but if we seek to discover the image of God in those about us, we are chiseling with the tools of the Infinite. Prof. Huxley says, "If there is no hope of a large improvement of the condition of the greater part of the human family, he would hail the advent of some kindly comet to sweep it all away." May Unity Club be forgiven for spending even a little time in discussing the question whether to do good to our neighbor is a fad.

In ancient times, men organized in war to work out blessings for the few – while today, we organize in peace to work out blessings for the many; and since women grace the civilization of all lands, what responsibility rests upon us collectively, upon us individually, upon us at the very hour. Science, which is the voice of God talking to us along the lines of natural law, says that the thirst of a daisy may change the depth of the Atlantic, so what we do and think today will somehow affect our neighbors in the Twentieth Century. It is well that we study household sanitation and all the appliances that may enable us to better protect our loved ones; but we propose to go farther. It may be said that a single sanitary law has accomplished more than all the achievements of private Philanthropy in a generation; and are not the altars of private Philanthropy continually wet with the tears of women? We have been the world's moral scavenger long enough. It is well to heal the bruises made by sin, but to prevent these bruises is far better.

Women are held responsible for much of the evil that exists, they always have, ever since Adam played the sneak in the garden, and they are responsible for much, especially for this that they do not claim the power to do good that should be theirs. Can you tell me what it is that makes good homes? What makes a church an influence for good, and makes private Philanthropy a blessing? Whatever this is, if it stops short of reaching the business life; if it does not take hold of the gambling table, the brothel and the saloon, then there is evidence that something is wrong. The power of one half the people stops short at a given point; it is not in touch with all the springs of its environment.

We sometimes complain that good laws are not enforced. Why are they not enforced? Because there are not enough people among those who are allowed to touch the levers – who want them enforced. Bishop Vincent, who has recently been in our city, in speaking publicly of the good things to be in the 20th Century, hoped that "aldermen will be honest and women will be contented." We believe nothing shows to us more clearly that the spirit of God is moving upon the hearts of his handmaidens than the fact that there exists this divine discontent.

Shall we who are mothers try to emulate the foolish virgins? In the great day that is coming, when the question will confront each one of us: "Where are the lambs committed to thy care in the wilderness of this world? We shall answer. Lord, it was not for me to follow them out upon the mountains, or into the valleys of temptation. It would have draggled my garments and made me displeasing to the world. So I staid and wrought in the tent. I pray thee excuse me, but the Angel with averted face passes her by."

George McDonald says, "No indulgence of passion destroys the spiritual nature so much as respectable selfishness." Let each one of us work along the line which to her seems to lead most directly towards this end of universal good.

One summer a few years ago, we took a stroll upon the banks of the dirty pool of partisan politics. We lingered long enough to meet a group of earnest spirits of whom Hamlin Garland was one of the coterie; and this is the thought he through in: "This great country is like an orange cut crosswise, each section leading to the center of things which is universal good. In each section are men at searching for the general good. At the circumference, we seem to be working alone, but as we approach the center, we begin to hear the sound of the pick axe of our neighbor working in his section, and we discover a great army coming in upon different lines."

In an age yet to be, and under a richer endowment of head and heart than now obtains, there may be men and women who can throw themselves with energy into every line of effort which leads upward, but not now. This Club seeks unity in diversity, and may it prove a fountain of intellectual and moral ideas, and not merely a channel through which the common stream runs.

"Mothers Duties and Privileges" (Undated)

We may have become mothers – God may have conferred upon us the dignity of being cocreators with him, and yet we may be among the most selfish of his creatures. Another idea widely prevalent is that motherhood brings with it unlimited powers and possibilities. We hear it from the lips of very excellent men and women that if mothers would do their whole duty, that society would soon become almost perfect. Indeed, Ruskin told the women of England that were it not for their selfishness, no war throughout Europe would last a week.

It seems to us the wiser plan to honestly recognize and admit our limitations. If it were true that mothers were given this stupendous power to regulate the world, what a wretched failure we have made of it. It would seem that there has been relegated to us a little more than half the molding power of forming the characters of our children, but I am not at all sure that a clearer view of the case would justify even our claim to this. Every child is the product of two parents; and in our puny efforts to think God's thoughts after him, let us be careful not to arrogate to ourselves and take away from man the responsibilities that are necessary to his prerogatives. The father and the mother, walking side by side, in the fear of God, equal in home government, equal in responsibility, will lead their flock out upon life's sunniest paths.

No, our children are not just what the mothers make them. Haven't we all heard the little story of the stock-breeder? He was a small ill-shapen man and some early excesses had helped to dwarf his growth, but he had a clear brain and practiced eye for improved stock. One day when he had just brought home a splendid Shorthorn of the male persuasion and was standing by the side of the mammoth animal. He said to him, "Well, you are a fine fellow." "Yes," said the Shorthorn, "so I am a fine fellow, and so would you have been if your parents had been selected with as much care as mine were." Then and there an idea entered the brains of the little stock man. He thought of his own family of four daughters, two of whom were well-built, sweet voiced and comely like their beautiful mother, and two of them were ill-shaped, weazen (?)-faced like himself – and a great wave of pity swept the soul of the little stock man as he thought how these innocent girls must go out into the world, with a physical heritage so pitiful. My sisters, we are formulating no creed – laying down no rules; but let us like Mary of old, ponder these things in our hearts.

We believe our first duty as human beings is to get ourselves, and keep ourselves in right relations to God. To do this demands honest thought and strong convictions and Nineteenth Century women of all others must have clear ideas of justice, purity, truth and love. Do we say that mothers are so busy, that the many little cares pressing us every day unfit us for sound thinking? Therefore, it is for us to accept the conclusions that the world has made for us and get along as best, we may. Do you ask why we insist upon the necessity for the best and highest thinking for mothers?

Because we have gone on in slipshod fashion long enough; because the struggle of life is on, and we would not work blindly. We must get up into the mount of vision or we cannot see the battle on the plains. It is that we may work out on the field of conflict the vision we have had in the mountains for whatever may be our ideals of life, or lack of ideals of life – they will manifest themselves in the details of the every day. As a man thinketh so is he. And, it is in our everyday life where the mother's power lies – for we teach our children more by what we are ourselves, than what we attempt to make them; and no day's record is lost. We are told by philosophers that the air set in motion by the first words of Adam and Eve in the Garden of Eden will continue to vibrate until the last trumpet sounds. No force for either good or bad but counts for something.

We do not believe that God has appointed to mothers a sphere and then left them defenseless in it. We mothers are slave to believe that to be able to "bring good gifts to our children," we must help ourselves. We must combat the false idea of woman that has made <u>sex</u> the paramount consideration. And what has the world's ill-balanced thought done for the mother even in the matter of <u>health</u>. It is said the Indian woman alights from her pony by the brook side – retires into the bushes, and soon returns with her new-born babe – washes it in the stream – wraps it in her blanket – remounts her pony and is ready next morning to pound the corn for her lazy brave. But she puts to shame our pale-faced invalidism.

It was a remark of a heathen sage that "God could not be everywhere, so he made mothers!" it is for us to know that the same code of morals is governing the life of our growing sons that we expect our daughters to live under. That it is not enough that our children have the purity of ignorance; but the purity of fire to consume the very suggestion of evil.

It is for mothers to demand that all discriminating restrictions in both church and state be removed before the oncoming feet of our young women, that the spirit of God poured out upon our sons and daughters may have free course and be glorified. It is for mothers to demand that a civilization that provides for thousands of women only the alternative of excessive toil for two or three dollars a week or charity, vice or starvation needs the mother spirit to ramify its every department.

And allow me to remind you the members of this noble organization which with a hand clasp of sympathy has so girdled the globe that the sun never sets upon you – what an inspiring opportunity opens before you to make the world better, along this special line. Your brilliant Ex-President in her address before your late convention in view of the possibility of dropping the franchise work said, "We are too far on this, our march towards political enfranchisement to return to swamps of indecision and the thickets of contentment with political serfdom."

May we all so prayerfully with our faces set towards our highest ideals and striving hard after them. This levelling down process that puts a premium upon vice by compelling a woman twenty years old to work for the wages of a boy of ten can be changed when women vote, for when men want office, they will be obliged to legislate in the interests of women. Let us teach our boys that every time a girl takes a place at less wages than a boy would just by so much does she drag down the wages of their fathers and brothers.

Finally, if it took twenty centuries of thinkers to culminate in a "Madam de Staet (?)" so we, the mothers of today from our high vantage ground if we do even all well as our foremothers, we must do a great deal better. But the future is full of promise. Away back in the beginning of civilization, when a man's possessions were in constant danger, and marauding was his occupation, and he went forth daily to imperil his life in defense of his home – the woman who remained in the hut, cave or castle had a sorry time; but today, the wolf is coming to dwell with the lamb, and the leopard to be down with the kid. When the marriage obligation has become so sacred that chastity and continence gain their rightful meaning, then -- a little child shall lead us.

"Notes on Old Age" (Undated)

When the venerable John Adams was asked how he had managed to preserve the vigor of his <u>mind</u> to such an advanced age, he replied, "Simply by exercising it!" Old minds are like horses; you must exercise them and you need to keep them in working order. The Rev. Daniel Waldo said, "A violent tempest of passion tears down the constitution more than a typhus fever."

Speaking of one of her birthdays, Mrs. Child says, "I count it something to know, that, though the flowers offered me were few, they were undoubtedly genuine. I never conformed much to the world's ways, but now that I am an old woman, I feel more free to ignore its conventional forms. That is a privilege. I deem it a great blessing, also, that the desire for knowledge grows more active, as the time for acquiring it diminishes, and I realize more fully how much there is to be learned. I want to know what every bird and insect is doing, and what it is done for. I peep and pry into their operation with more and more interest the older I grow; but they keep their own secrets so well that I discover very little. What I do find out, however, confirmed my belief that the hand that made them is Divine."

"But the most valuable compensations of age are those of a spiritual character. I have committed so many faults myself that I have become more tolerant on others than I was when I was young. My restless <u>aspirations</u> are quieted. Having arrived at this state of peacefulness and submissions, I find the last few years the happiest of my life!"

"Poor Stupid Uncle Sam" (Undated)

(Author's note: Pages 1-3 of her handwritten copy are missing.)

Poor stupid Uncle Sam. He fails to see that the laws made for women a hundred and fifty years ago have not yielded to women's growth, and she is resisting the chains which confine her, and therefore the home, her special realm, is the loser.

What means the enormous number of divorce suits brought by women which now burden our courts until your souls are sick with every day's report. Does it mean that men are more cruel – more drunken – more licentious than fifty years ago? Is it the fault of our loose divorce laws? I believe the cause is deeper than any or all of these. Women's ideal of excellence is raised; and the conditions written and unwritten which marriage imposes – the authority over the wife – the children which are hers as well as his -- his control of the earnings she helps to acquire – all this power had men take advantage of, and through this cause more than all others. Is the American home being sacrificed?

Fifty years ago, the poor woman who starved and was beaten by a drunken husband would still cling to his beastly self, while every two years or more often she added another drunkard's child to the wretched group at her knee; today this woman would rise up in her stronger selfhood and walk out of his house forever. Today for a man to make as good a husband as his grandfather, he must make a great deal better one. Let Uncle Sam give to every mother, wife and daughter the same political freedom enjoyed by his man subjects and women could adjust themselves to their conditions, or make conditions to which they could adjust themselves with a facility which Uncle Sam never dreamed of.

Again, what robbery of women he allows. The tax on tea which our forefathers fought to the death to resist was only about $1500 a year, while women are every year robbed of millions. Call it by whatever name, we will – we, tax paying women are the slaves of voting men. Again, Uncle Sam is a marvelous liar. Every principle of freedom which he has enunciated for 150 years but emphasizes the claims of women to representation in a government that pretends to be by the consent of the governed.

How does he treat a woman who attempts to make a home upon his public domains? Let her stay nearly five years upon a claim, but if she marries in the meantime, which all the world advises her to do, what happens? She forfeits her claim to the land. In the National Cemetery at Pittsburg Landing, of the 3594 graves, all have been marked by marble tablets except those of the four female Army nurses who lost their lives through diseases contracted in the service; and this distinction was by instructions from the War Department.

Each state is allowed to make such restrictions against women as the men of that state may decide. Iowa boasts of its absolute equality in matters of property. In the case of a certain excellent lady of Des Moines — a member of the Presbyterian church — her husband's acts becoming unbearable, they lived apart, he entering into a written contract with him to pay her a monthly stipend. This he soon failed to pay and the wife brought suit – but the Supreme Court of the state decided that a contract between man and wife "was against public policy," and today in Iowa it is not a crime for a man to defraud his wife.

A friend told me of a case in another state which came under her own observation. Two young people married poor and soon after the husband by an accident became a permanent invalid. The wife while nursing carefully her husband, also did washing until she had accumulated enough to buy a house and a few acres of ground, the deed to which from the force of public opinion was made in the husband's name. After fifteen years, the husband died, and his relatives took two thirds of the property allowing to the wife the use of one third while she lived and at her death all went to his relatives.

In several states, the married mother still has little more legal right to her child than a cow has to her calf. If a wife has property in her own name and sells it for cash – if the husband should receive the money in his own hands, he may spend it, and there is no federal or state law that will compel him to restore to her.

A little scrap of history came to my knowledge just the other day which shows how our children suffer by the lack of the mother influence in public affairs. When the University of Iowa was founded by President Jefferson, of course it was only intended for the education of boys, and all possible inducements were offered to the young men to attend; and among others were accommodations provided in the building by which women were to be sacrificed to the passions of these young men. If one mother had been on the Board of Trustees of that University, could such things have been?

The heritage of power is a curse to men as well as to women. I think we women are given too much to look to men to do the work which we should do ourselves. If we ever hope to set ourselves right with the world, it is for each of us to be faithful in these matters as they come up before us as in the every day.

Portland, Oregon (1905)

We bring you a word tonight from that broad plateau which is drained by the three great rivers of the country, with the giant Rockies on one side and the mighty Alleghenies on the other – the states of the Middle West lean smilingly to the southland's sunny slopes. With their rich deposits of metals and coal, with their wooded hills and sparkling streams – and with a soil so generous that if you tickle it with a hoe, it will laugh with the harvest; we are confident that it is the very spot where God stood when he said, "Let there be light."

In this great struggle for the freedom of women, the Middle West is trying to do its honorable share. In some of these states, I speak especially of Iowa, the state of my adoption; the women who are asking for political liberty have for thirty years regularly come to our legislative fig tree only to find that the time of figs is not yet. The politicians do not want a class of voters introduced upon whom they cannot count and the stave off our appeal as long as possible. Our state is overwhelmingly Republican, but the other day, a well informed, ambitious gentleman of that party said to me, "There is no danger that the granting of woman suffrage would injure the dominant party in Iowa and they might just as well give the ballot to women as not."

All this time the people are being educated. Today, there are counties in Iowa where a man dare not stand for the legislature unless he is first known to stand for the political rights of women. When the master of the universe has points to carry in his government, he impresses his will in the structure of minds. The women of these states have determined that they will have the ballot granted to them even if they have to born and raise the men to do it. The scheme is already begun. Other women have done far more, but I have myself been privileged to raise three sons to manhood representing eighteen feet of woman suffrage dyed in the wool.

It requires a fine effort of the imagination to see an evil that surrounds us on every side. Uncle Sam is good and generous, but stiff and stupid and dreadfully slow to see that women can help him. He reminds us of Bishop Niles of New Hampshire who, while attending an Episcopal Convention in Boston, was one day seated in the public garden on one of the low settees. The Bishop is a very heavy man and when he attempted to rise, he found great difficulty in regaining his feet. In the midst of his struggle, a wee tot of a girl came along and offered to help him. The Bishop had ceased trying to rise and, looking critically at the little girl, told her that she could not. "Well," said the little girl finally, "I've helped Grandpa lots of times when he was lots drunker than you are."

It is claimed that no country is easily governed whose territory lies chiefly north and south; and Kipling says, "There is never a law of God or man sans (?) north of fifty three." There is a great unrest up and down this valley plateau; an unrest that will not down at the behest of politicians. The same unrest that stirs the Russian peasant to revolt, and made of our Revolutionary fathers slayers of men. It is as great an injustice to a man to make him a tyrant as to make him a slave. The women of the Middle West are realizing that their duty to their husbands and sons demands that they should secure the ballot – and let a woman once get a vision of duty, and she will rise up early and lie down later.

Does the time seem long? It took Copernicanism two or three hundred years to overthrow the Ptolemaic system, and between the time of Nero whose first steam engine revolved in the Serapion (?) until James Watts made possible our ocean liners was period of twenty centuries.

Manhood suffrage to achieve its present proportions has been over six hundred years in the making. Woman suffrage has been agitated less than seventy. But the women of the Middle West are neither sighing nor crying. The day has gone by when for women to weep over their wrongs. Our country is prosperous. Women share in this prosperity. We no longer talk about the schools being open to us. We make the schools. We take the goods the gods provide, believing that if we remain underlings, it is not in our stars but in ourselves. To doubt is to be disloyal.

In this great battle for freedom, there is no bugle to ever sound retreat for the women of the Middle West, "We are coming father Abraham, six hundred thousand more."

"Then and Now," National American Woman Suffrage Association Convention

Some of us who happen to be extant during the early part of the 19th Century have a vivid recollection of the contrast between the then and now; especially the contrast in the condition of women. But we would go back further than our own memory takes us and glance for a moment of history, but as history records chiefly the exploits of men, we should say we will glance a moment at his story.

Through all the creeping centuries, woman has been the quiet, the unknown, the uncomplaining, the oppressed. Indeed, she has been profoundly thankful that she was permitted to be created at all; for from the record in Genesis, she has always had the suspicion that if Adam had happened to be satisfied to be alone, and willing to tend the garden himself, that our much maligned foremother would not have been made. But as to when or where our humanity started, we are not concerned; whether it were upon the banks of the Euphrates, upon the shores of the Nile, or in the valley of the St. Laurence, for the scientist and the biologist assure us that when the first Anthropoid ape made a nest in the forks of a tree, then and there our civilization began.

In a far off age, the primitive father was the hunter and fighter, and but little more. The primitive neither tended the cave or the hut; she tanned the skins for clothing, dug the ground for the maize, cared for the springs of water, she trained the dogs to help carry the burdens while the men strode on before.

She watched the example of a bird, bee and beast and slowly discovered the rudiments of what has become the splendid civilization of today. She was the origin of the town and the city, and was the means by which church, school and society came into existence.

Women were the founders of the world's homes, and through all the ages have been their protecting spirit, and no powers of earth are strong enough to drive out of their natures the love of home, though in these later days, thousands of men and some women are apparently frightened almost to death with the fear that if women are not restricted by law, they will get out of the home.

The primitive mother would seek a safe place for her young and defend them by tooth or claw. It is in the same mother spirit coming down through the evolving and refining centuries that today, in the cult of 20th century is asking for the legal power to protect these homes. That the U.S. Congress and some state legislatures have put themselves in the way of the world's oncoming movement for woman's freedom is just a little eddy in the current; only an incident in the sweep of progress. Indeed, the persistency of politicians to arrest this movement seems to add to the gaiety of nations.

A few years ago, in one of our western states during a session of its legislature when the House of Representatives had just voted down a woman suffrage bill, immediately about one hundred women rose and left the hall to hold an indignation meeting in the corridor. Feeling ran very high; but upon the face of one of the leading spirits was a look of supreme satisfaction. The chairman of this improvised meeting said to her, "Mrs. Blank, why do you look so happy?" She answered, "I am thinking of the men we have just left in the hall. Although their action in its stupid injustice was almost enough to make the very stones in the street cry out, yet they sat in their seats erect, clean, well clothed. Think what an advance they have made over their great, great, grinning ancestors, hanging by their tails in the trees."

Conditions which obtained even a hundred years ago are today in the minds of women simply intolerable. We remember even fifty years ago how a sympathizing clergy would advise and console women; they would conjure them to be content in the position in which they said, "Divine Providence had been pleased to place them." They were told that if they would continue patient and steadfast to the end that after a few more sighs and a few more tears, they would all be wafted into Abraham's bosom. As a little girl, I used to wonder what kind of a place of rest this bosom would be to which my mother was expected to go.

Today, even Heaven must bid higher for the souls of women. For today, each woman of us would demand the whole of Abraham's bosom to herself nor divide up with Sarah or Hager.

The day for women to walk through the world with bowed heads and weeping eyes has passed by. We have quit crying. What good do our tears do? Women have come to the same conclusion as the eminent Professor of Chemistry, who, after a quarrel with his wife, and she had burst into tears, taking up his hat to leave the house, said to her, "Emily, your tears do no good at all; they are only common water, with a small percentage of phosphorous salts and a trace of chloride of sodium."

Fainting too is at a discount. Seventy-five years ago, no function in polite society was complete without a fainting woman. A New York specialist declared that he used to visit a score of fainting woman every twenty-four hours. Today, our most refined and cultured young women, with faces unveiled, and fore-arms bared, take a walk of five miles or ten and come swinging home with their cheeks wearing natural roses. Our matrons too grow old slowly. Even staid members of this Association, women of 60 may be seen <u>sprinting</u> to the street cars almost any day.

When the world was young, fifty centuries of time brought less change in woman's lot than comes to her now in fifty years. We have all the experience of the past to aid us. The very stars in their courses are working for us. We have gained nearly everything. We will gain all. Man suffrage crept along through more than six centuries to reach its present proportion. Comparing our gains with his, woman suffrage since its first inception has come forward with the speed of the whirl-wind.

For the over-burdened woman, we have sympathy – for the wicked woman, we have charity – but of the discouraged woman, we are ashamed. But even in these happier days there are some things which have been left over from pre-historic times; and among these is the antisuffrage woman. There are not many of her who are active, or seem to be really alive. A few rare specimens have been observed upon the Atlantic seaboard, two or three in the Middle West, but beyond to the Rocky Mountains and the Pacific Ocean, there are almost no formations of this character.

Some social biologists claim that she is the product of the stone age. But she is here – in limited numbers and the liquor interests of this country especially are ready to do her honor. The antisuffrage man or woman whether he or she knows it or not are trying to do for the politics of this nation precisely what the corporate liquor interests of the country would like to have them do. They would help to prolong the day for the corporate liquor interests of the country to coin money from the blood and tears of women and little children. The saloon can stand up boldly before an army of good men; but it would cower before an army of good men reinforced by an army of good women with ballots in their hands.

A pressing problem today is the immigrant. In vast numbers they come to us and in them the prejudices of the old world meet here the corrupter and political chicanery of the new world, and they are often voted in herds under the manipulation of American bosses. My friends, we must get up into the mount of vision or we can not see the battle that rages in the plain. It is a battle royal against the forces of greed, political corruption and corporate power. But the immigrant is eager to learn, and this wonderful country of ours has in it the machinery and the institutions to Americanize the immigrant and control and humanize our own people. And we will. The muck rake is abroad in the land and the terror of public execration is lashing the dishonest. The forces of good are stronger than the forces of evil.

The men and the women, the fathers and the mothers will together work out our country's salvation.

"God's in his heaven. All's right with the world."

(Author's note: Coggeshall's speech was a headliner for a Chicago newspaper, and the text repeated here to indicate the editor's selections from the speech.)

SOBS OUT OF STYLE
Woman Who Weeps Is Declared Behind Times
Suffragists Say Wife Should Not be Too Good Natured
Convention Reelects Rev. Anna Howard Shaw as Its President

"The day for women to walk through the world with bowed heads and weeping eyes has passed by. Women are no longer the uncomplaining, oppressed creatures whose only cause to be thankful is that they are alive."

Thus was the progress of womankind set forth my Mrs. Mary J. Coggeshall of Des Moines, Iowa, at last evening's session of the convention of the National American Woman's Suffrage Association at the Music Hall. The feminine audience that filled the auditorium showed by its repeated applause that it was in hearty accord with her sentiments.

"Throughout the centuries, the woman has been the quiet, the uncomplaining, the oppressed," said Mrs. Coggeshall. "Indeed, she has cause to be thankful that she has been created at all. For from the record in Genesis she has always had the suspicion that if Adam happened to be satisfied alone and willing to tend the garden himself our much-maligned foremother would not have been made."

"Even in these happier days there are some things left over from prehistoric times. Among these is the anti-suffrage woman. A few rare specimens have been observed on the Atlantic seaboard and there are a few in the middle west, but beyond the Rocky Mountains there are no such formations visible. Some social biologists claim that she is the product of the stone age."

"We cry no more and fainting is at a discount. Sixty years ago no society function was complete without a fainting woman. Even fifty years ago a sympathizing clergy would devise and console women by conjuring them to be content in the position in which Divine Providence had placed them. They were told that if they continue penitent and steadfast to the end that after a few more sighs and a few more tears they would all be wafted to Abraham's bosom."

"Now even Heaven must bid higher for the souls of women, for today each one of us would demand the whole of Abraham's bosom for herself, not even dividing it up with Sarah and Hagar."

(Author's note: Jake was somewhat puzzled by the statement about "Abraham's bosom." The story in Genesis about Sarah and Hagar is fairly well known. Sarah was the wife of Abraham and Hagar was Sarah's servant. Sarah could not conceive so gave Hagar to Abraham, in accordance with the custom of the day. Hagar did conceive and then Sarah turned negative on Hagar, etc. Jake thought that being wafted into Abraham's bosom had something to do with a promise to women in the Bible. That was not the case, but ministers must have assured righteous women of that eventuality as indicated by Mary Jane.)

Iowa Editor Responses

Mary Jane Whiteley Coggeshall impresses us as one who was empirically oriented. From the files in the Schlesinger Library, Radcliffe Institute, Harvard University was recorded that in 1882, as Chairman of the Executive Committee of the Iowa Suffrage Society, she had written a brief letter to the editors of 154 newspapers in Iowa and one in Omaha, Nebraska. The base letter enquired whether the editor would "advocate or allow to be advocated an amendment to the Iowa state constitution giving all citizens equal rights and privileges regardless of sex." Afterward, she tabulated the responses concerning woman suffrage and other rights into three classifications: (1) "Yes" – 105; (2) "Neutral" – 24; and (3) "No" – 26.

While Mary Jane may have been somewhat pleased that two-thirds of the responses were positive, readers may wonder why the 26 editors were negative. Why deny women the right to the ballot? The first two "No" examples provide samples of the letter she wrote. Presumably the letters to the other 153 newspapers were similar to the first two.

The Next Ism
State Press

We are in receipt of note:

Des Moines, Iowa
June 29, 1882
Iowa State Press

Dear Sir:
Now that the smoke of the battle for prohibition has cleared away, and recognizing that the power of the press in molding public opinion, the executive committee of the Iowa woman suffrage society wish to know whether you will advocate or allow to be advocated in your columns an amendment to the state constitution giving all citizens equal rights and privileges regardless of sex.

Yours very respectfully,
Mary J. Coggeshall
Chairman, Ex. Com.

No, we will not advocate it, nor permit its advocacy in our columns. The woman suffrage agitation has accomplished all the good that can come of it, in liberalizing our statutes as to the property and personal rights of women. This, so far as we know, was the sole object had in view by all the sensible people who ever gave aid and comfort to woman suffrage, and since its accomplishment they have left the agitation of the question to a few fanatics and preachers. Woman now occupies a position superior to man, with more rights and privileges and comforts than he enjoys, and we see no need of depriving her of all this by giving her the ballot and introducing her into politics. During the late prohibitory campaign the women took part, led by the preachers, and closed their efforts by appearing at the polls to bribe voters with tea, coffee and biscuits. We think now that the curtain is rung down on that sort of thing it would be better stay down. Women with the ballot means a female party led by the preachers, and the clergy have too much power here anyway, and are using it to subvert our form of government, to which they are opposed because as yet the law does not guarantee to them possession of saddle, bridal, whip and spur wherewith to ride mankind.

To conclude, we have too much respect for woman in her modesty and her purity to sully either by dragging her into politics, and we have too much respect for pure religion and undefiled to increase the power of the preachers who are already disgusting mankind with everything sacred.

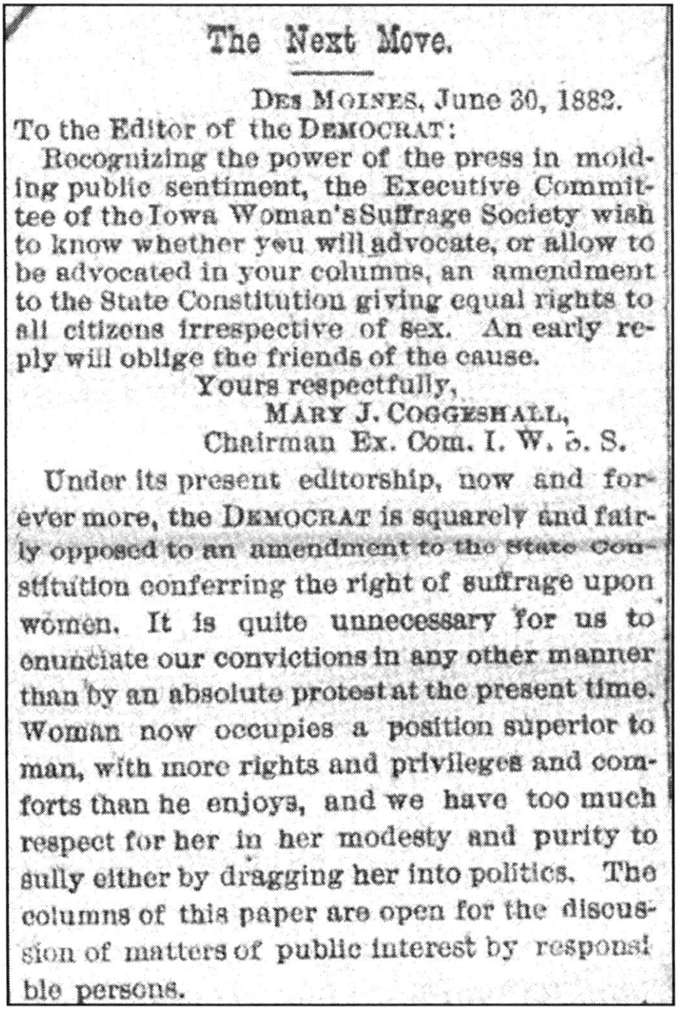

**Fig. 4 Newspaper clippping. (Source: Schlesinger Library, Radcliffe In-
stitute, Harvard University).**

(Author's note: The name of the newspaper was illegible.)

A woman in Des Moines writes to us to know if, having successfully
adopted the Prohibitory Amendment, the Journal will advocate woman
suffrage, or allow others to do so through its columns. It is our opinion that,
until the Prohibitory Amendment business is finally, and definitely settled,
there is undue haste to immediately urge this matter, -- that if the measure
is carried out as its friends hope it may be, there will be less reason why
suffrage for women be demanded, -- and finally, that the great majority of
the best women of the State; -- the wives, mothers and sisters who deserve

the love, honor and respect of their relatives – do not want, and will use their influence, to prevent its being made a part of our constitutional law. In fifteen years' residence in Iowa, during which time we have heard this matter discussed, we have found the number of good worthy women who demand the ballot to be exceedingly small, and are firm in the belief that there are ten men who would favor such a measure where there is one lovable woman. We would not be understood that there are no good women who would demand the ballot, because such is not the fact, but their number is exceedingly small as compared to the number who are not. And finally, we believe the politics and policy of Iowa would not be increased for good if she were armed with the ballot. Whenever we are satisfied that women in the aggregate, want the ballot, and that it would be of benefit for good to themselves, or the State at large, we will advocate its adoption – until then, we'll think about it.

In the other 23 negative responses, Mary Jane either saved the handwritten letters or copied them. None were newspaper clippings. In the above three negative editorials were mentioned (1) too much power for women and the clergy, (2) the majority of women are against the Amendment, (3) women would be "sullied into politics," (4) suffragettes are not responsible persons and (5) suffragettes are not "good worthy women." In the other 23 negative editorials, (1), (2) and (3) were mentioned. To round out the "Top 10," the additional reasons were (6) purity of the home will be compromised, (7) the local brewing industry may be harmed, (8) the Constitution has too many amendments, (9) the suffrage issue is not appropriate for this newspaper and (10) the women in this country are not Amazons.

Following are other samples of the negative responses:

Lyon County Reporter, Rock Rapids

The Amendment referred to we believe is one which cannot and will not pass. The majority of the sex which it so nearly concerns, would not support the move. We believe that women should have the same rights as their opposites, but if they do not choose to use them, what is the need of changing a constitution which as yet has not abused them. There is one question which admits of a difference of opinion and that is the educational question. We believe that the right of suffrage should be extended and used in all matters pertaining to educational interests. Farther than that we cannot support the move.

Postville Review

I have no space at present to devote to woman suffrage pro or con. It will be time enough after another legislature passes upon it to agitate that question. As ever, I am unalterably opposed to the measure and when the proper time comes I shall be most happy to discuss the question with you. At present there are more important matters to attend to.

Bloomfield Democrat

I will allow any respectable person to advocate woman suffrage in the Democrat within reasonable limits, provided that the space used is paid for at my regular rates for local advertising, 3 cents per line.

Dallas County Democrat

Yours of the 16th at hand. We have carefully noted its contents and the implied request therein and in reply have to say that as the editors of this paper are divided on the question, we are compelled to ignore the subject in the columns of the paper until we can agree.

Boone County Gazette

We have always been opposed to Womans Suffrage believing the same both unwise and injudicious in the abstract. We are always willing to help women in all their legitimate efforts and acknowledging their powerful assistance in the noble work of the Amendment, are unwilling to bring them in the whirlpool of political strife.

These views are the result of long reflecting.

We respectfully refuse your proposition. Not believing in the principle unless it can be carried out to the whole extent to which men are responsible, which we think is impossible, as the women of this country are not Amazons. Another reason is we depend upon the whole community here for the support of our brewers, and cannot take a decided step on either side.

You will doubtless meet with better success at Calamino (?) 5 miles east of this place. There is a new paper started there called the Calamino (?) Enterprise. The editor is a woman's rights man and a Spiritualist and Free Thinker.

More Reflections on Mary Jane Whiteley Coggeshall

(Author's note: Jake's third cousin, Cynde Coggeshall Fanter, of Des Moines, IA has been very helpful in assembling information on her remarkable great grandmother. Following are selections from her paper for a club called Porteus, a description of the historic Boone Suffrage Parade in 1908, and a legal procedure on woman's right to vote on funding a city hall in Des Moines also in 1908 (Fanter, 2016)).

<u>Selections from "Quiet and Not so Quiet" about Mary Jane Coggeshall (Fanter, 2012)</u>

In the fall of 1870, the Polk County, Iowa, Woman Suffrage Society was organized. One of it's charter members and officers was Mary Jane Coggeshall. Earlier, she recalled how lonely she felt when "… a few women unknown to each other walked their daily rounds of domestic duties with the thought in the minds of each other that 'I alone of all the women in this young city believe in the equality of women with men.'" With membership in this Society, she was no longer lonely, having found a mission to which she could and did dedicate the balance of her life.

For many years Mary Jane was the editor of "The Woman's Hour" and later "The Woman's Standard," weekly newspapers established to spread the suffrage message. She was president of the Iowa Suffrage Association in 1890-91 and 1903-05 and honorary president from 1906-11. She was the first Iowa member of the National American Woman Suffrage Association and for years was the only board member west of the Mississippi.

An historian of the Iowa movement, Mary Ankeny Hunter, commented about Mary Jane, "The record does not include the hundreds of committee meetings of both county and state societies, the parlor meetings in her home, the countless speeches delivered through each year, the use of her spare bedroom and food served from her table to suffrage workers; the terms she served as an officer of the Political Equity Club (Author's note: By 1920, it became "The Mary Jane Coggeshell Club" – The Des Moines Register, Nov. 10, 1920); the continued support she gave to every form of money raising; the political acumen she employed in every legislative campaign throughout the years. Nor does it include the testimony as to the quality of public speeches and newspaper articles concerning the woman's rights questions; she was exceptionally gifted in logical, persuasive, and convincing argument, combined with wit and beauty of diction."

By 1908, she did see additional vigor in the movement with the Boone Suffrage Parade and a favorable decision by the Iowa Supreme Court described in the following pages. Even so, Mary Jane Coggeshall, at 71 in 1908, was displaying some discouragement. She said, "We who have toiled up the steps of the old Capitol only to see our bills defeated upon final vote. We who took our baby boys with us to those early meetings, now find these boys are voters, while their mothers are still asking for freedom. We only hope the next generation of women may find their work made easier because we have trodden the path before them."

The Boone Suffrage Parade

Boone, Iowa is located about 40 miles northwest of Des Moines. What happened there was a national and even international event for woman's suffrage. Dr. Suzanne Caswell, an historian, described this event as follows:

The year 1908 marked a turning point for the American's woman's suffrage movement across the country. The three suffrage parades which took place during that year – one in the East in New York City, one in the West in Oakland, California, and one in the Midwest in Boone, Iowa – reflecting the changing climate in the American suffrage movement and helped to dramatically refocus and define that movement for the decade which followed, eventually culminating in the passage of the Nineteenth Amendment (Caswell, 2008).

Rev. Eleanor Elizabeth Gordon recalled the summer of 1908 in Des Moines (Gordon, 2008).

Perhaps the dreariest of all the dreary meetings of the summer were the monthly meetings of the Des Moines Political Equality Club. No matter how hot and dusty the day and night might be, dear Mrs. Coggeshall would not consent to a single adjourned session. I remember particularly the August meeting of the Club. Even a salamander would have been tired of the heat by August if he lived in Iowa. That day, following a hot night, had brought me about to the limit of my strength and courage. Eight or ten faithful souls were present. It was loyalty to Mrs. Coggeshall that brought us together rather than an interest in the meetings. We listened to an earnest paper written by an earnest woman, read in an earnest manner, giving good and sufficient reasons why women were entitled to vote.

After the meeting, Rev. Gordon, President of the State Association, concerned about the viability of the movement contacted the President of the Boone Suffrage Club where the State Convention was to be held in the fall. The President was of the same state of mind. Rev. Gordon suggested, "Why not have a parade? Why not attempt something different, even if we are accused of imitating the English Militants?" That was decided and the details were left with the President.

There were cautions about staging such a demonstration. Even Mary Jane Coggeshall along with others were not supportive. On the morning before the event in the center of Boone, IA, Rev. Gordon assured Mary Jane that she need not join the parade. She replied, "If the delegates of this convention march, I shall go, " she said in that gentle voice that with all its gentleness could be so firm and decided, as Rev. Gordon recalled.

Fig. 5 The Boone parade passes the First Methodist Church. The taller woman on the right leading the marchers may have been Mary Jane Whiteley Coggeshall according to Cynde Coggeshall Fanter. (Source: Trail Tales, The Journal of Boone County History, Summer/Fall 2008, No. 110, Boone County Historical Society, Boone, IA)

After the parade, accolades came from the city of Boone. One woman, whose husband had doubts earlier, reported to Rev. Gordon, "My husband says that the parade today has done more to advance the cause of political equality in Boone than all the Suffrage clubs, all the conventions, all the lectures and debates have ever done. He says there was but one topic of conversation this afternoon in the homes, shops, offices and stores and on the street, and that was suffrage for women."

Following is a concession by Mary Jane Coggeshall in her remarks before the parade:

"Thank you, Reverend Gordon. You are very kind. As always, it is an honor to be in the presence of so many wonderful, intelligent and dedicated women. I must tell you that it is invigorating to think we are about to step into an historic parade for the cause we have been working for these many years. I must also confess that when Reverend Gordon first proposed such a parade to our Unity Circle group several months ago, I was not convinced that it was best for our cause. I frankly worried that such a step was too radical and would not be a dignified expression of our sentiments. I was worried that the country was not ready for such a novel activity; and that we might well lose ground after working so hard these many decades to get where we are today. I had no doubt in the prospect of a positive response to this new approach. I admit I voted against having this parade.

Now, as you well know and as I have many times spoken, I have an unshakeable faith in the democratic rule of the majority. We must remain united and speak with one voice if ever we are to achieve our goal. I therefore willingly yield to the majority will and join with you in a new expression of our unfailing dedication to the just cause that brings us here today. I choose to march today, not without doubts about the wisdom of a parade that some may see as undignified and unworthy of our sex and perhaps compromising of our goal, but with dedication to the principles of the democratic majority ruled society which we so earnestly wish to join as political equals. Ladies, let us march with one voice!"

Letter to Iowa Senator J.E. Clark, April 1886

(Author's note: The letter was in the possession of Lydia Whitely Ferris, sister of Mary Jane Whiteley Coggeshall.)

The Iowa Woman Suffrage Society

Des Moines Iowa, April 1886
Sen. J.E. Clark

Dear Sir:

The friends of Municipal Woman Suffrage are led to infer that the Special Com. upon that subject in the Iowa Senate, has absolved itself from the responsibility of reporting to that body either for, or against the measure by transferring its consideration to the Judiciary Com.; which is its probable grave.

You no doubt conceive that it is unconstitutional, and we know the "Opinion" of the Atty. Gen'l. For your honest convictions we have a genuine respect; but it would be absurd to suppose that the friends of the measure throughout the state who have thought much, and sacrificed much, in order to bring this matter before the attention of the legislature, supported by the petitions of a vast number of interested persons, will serenely acquiesce in the decisions of the few. Otherwise men decide that under our Constitution not only municipal, but complete suffrage can be granted to women by act of Legislature.

The suffragists have felt somewhat aggrieved that those to whom of all others in the state we have looked for warmest support in this matter, should refuse to entertain any argument in its favor that could be brought by its friends. It will be a most painful conviction to have to be brought home to the various county and township suffrage organizations; the fact that some of the leading temperance politicians of Iowa occupy common ground with the brewers and saloon keepers in opposition to their claims. In view of the many who are looking to this plan as a speedy and final escape from the rule of the rum power, it is hoped you will be very careful to stifle no promptings of your own conscience or ignore the feeling of justice in the minds of others.

Very Respectfully
Mary J. Coggeshall

Mary J. Coggeshall, et al v. City of Des Moines, 1908

This court case involving Mary Jane Coggeshall is highlighted in a display at the Iowa Bar Association headquarters in Des Moines, IA (Fanter, 2016).

At a city election the question whether the City of Des Moines should erect a city hall at a cost of not to exceed $350,000 was on the ballot. Two of the four female plaintiffs appeared at the polls, requested ballots and were denied the right to vote. The proposal carried by a majority of 729 votes. The council procured plans and specifications, purchased a site, authorized a contract to superintend construction, levied taxes and intended to issue and sell bonds. At this point, William H. Baily and Grace H. Ballantyne commenced an action on behalf of the four female plaintiffs asking an injunction and that the election be declared void. The district court refused to so hold, and Mr. Baily and Grace Ballantyne appealed to the Supreme Court of Iowa which reversed and held the election was void because women as a class were barred from voting. Various constitutional and statutory provisions were analyzed by the court. Defendants contended that even if some women were refused the right to vote, thereby the election was not invalidated. The court observed that Grace H. Ballantyne was the attorney for the Political Equality Club of 150 women and she had been told by the city solicitor that in his opinion women were not entitled to vote. This was reported to the Federation of Women's Clubs with 1,200 members and publicity was given to the fact that women would not be entitled to vote. The court noted that according to the last State census, there were 19,179 native born women above 21 years of age in Des Moines which was 741 more than the men. The court said, "… no time need be wasted in deducing from this proof that more qualified voters than were necessary to overcome the majority resided in the city June 20, 1907, the date of the election."

Special section of the Des Moines Register in 1969

In the archives of The Des Moines Register on Sunday, November 2, 1969 in a special tribute to suffragettes, they identified Martha Callanan and Mary Jane Coggeshall of Des Moines as "keen-witted Quaker women." This fits with Jake's claim that Quakers were instrumental in the movement, even in Iowa. However, one might have difficulty interpreting the subsequent reservation, "These women were good intentioned, too, and whether their weakness was feminine or merely a human quality can be debated."

Suffrage Memorabilia and States Granting Women's Rights

(Author's note: In the boxes of the archives of Mary Jane Whiteley Coggeshall in the Schlesinger Library, Radcliffe Institute, Harvard University were memorabilia she saved in addition to her speeches, editors' responses to her petition for support and newspaper clippings. Prominent were the flags with four stars, pins with her picture with Anna Howard Shaw (Fig.6) and numerous ribbons from conventions.)

Anna Howard Shaw

Following a much varied life including preaching as a Methodist minister and receiving a medical degree from Boston College, Anna Howard Shaw became active in the suffrage movement in around 1886 (Wikipedia, "Anna Howard Shaw"). From 1904 to 1915, Shaw was president of the National American Woman Suffrage Association and was on the program of the 1908 Boone Suffrage Parade.

In the headline of the article in a Chicago paper entitled "SOBS OUT OF STYLE" featuring Coggeshall's address to the NAWSA in 1907 was the announcement that the "Convention Reelects Rev. Anna Howard Shaw as its President." Conceivably, the pin might have represented Coggeshall's support of Shaw's reelection as she was not only a speaker but also a delegate to that convention.

A brief recount of Shaw's life is deserving (Wikipedia, "Anna Howard Shaw."). Born in Newcastle-upon-Tyne, UK, in 1847, she and her family moved to Massachusetts when she was four. When she was twelve, her father "took up a claim" of 360 acres in northern Michigan and sent her mother and her with four siblings to secure the claim alone. It was a desolate place and Anna had to help her struggling mother and the other children in a primitive setting.

Her education included Big Rapids High School and Albion College in Michigan and Boston University School of Theology in 1876; then an M.D. at Boston University in 1886. Her legacy includes the Anna Howard Shaw Women's Center at Albion College and the Anna Howard Shaw Center at the Boston University School of Theology. She died on July 2, 1919 at age 72 only a few months before Congress ratified the Nineteenth Amendment to the US Constitution.

The Four Starred Flag

The flag represents the Iowa Equal Suffrage Association's effort for full enfranchisement in the states which only four states had achieved by 1896. First was the Wyoming territory in 1869, the Utah territory in 1870, Colorado in 1893 and Idaho in 1896 (Wikipedia, "Timeline of women's suffrage in the United States.") The fifth state was Washington in 1910, so the flags were relevant between 1896 and 1910.

From 1911 to 1916, six additional western states granted unconditional suffrage to women. It was not until 1917 that an eastern state (New York) voted for full suffrage followed by Oklahoma, and South Dakota. In 1919, the same privileges were granted by Michigan, Oklahoma and South Dakota before the US Nineteenth Amendment in 1920.

Ribbons

An example of Mary Jane Coggeshall's extensive involvement in the suffrage movement in Iowa is depicted on the ribbon for the Thirty-sixth Annual Convention of the Iowa Equal Suffrage Association in Des Moines in 1907. The ribbons in these next pages illustrate her wide national reach to state conventions in Missouri and Michigan and national conventions of the NAWSA in Grand Rapids, MI (1899), Minneapolis, MN (1901), New Orleans, LA (1903) and Chicago, IL (1907). In addition, she reported on the NAWSA annual meetings in Washington, DC (1904), Portland, OR (1905), where she also spoke, and Seattle, WA (1909).

Fig. 6 The Four Starred Flag, Pin with pictures of Anna Howard Shaw and Mary Jane Whiteley Coggeshall and flag from the 1907 State Convention. (Source: Schlesinger Library, Radcliffe Institute, Harvard University for the above illustration and the ribbons on the following page).

FOR PRESIDENT

SENATOR W.S. ALLISON

OF IOWA.

ST. LOUIS, MISSOURI
1896.

Mo.E.S.A.
Convention
Oct. 17, 18, '98
ST. JOSEPH, MO.

ANNUAL
CONVENTION
WOMAN'S
STATE SUFFRAGE

ASSOCIATION,
DES MOINES, IA.
OCT. 15TH, 1897.

DELEGATE
N.A.W.S.A.
31st ANNUAL
CONVENTION
April 27...
... to ...
May 3, '99
GRAND RAPIDS,
MICH.

N.
A.
W.
S.
A.
MINNEAPOLIS,
1901.

AUDITOR
N.
A.
W.
S.
A.
NEW ORLEANS.
1903.

Twenty-first Annual
Convention
Michigan
Equal
Suffrage
Association
Port Huron
October 21 to November 1
1905

DELEGATE
N
A
W
S
A
CHICAGO
1907

Rights of women and children by state in 1908

Among Coggeshall's archives was this incredible tabulation of the legislation in the four states compiled by Catherine Waugh McCulloch entitled "SOME LAWS OF AN IDEAL STATE WHICH PROTECT WOMEN AND CHILDREN." All items are for the four states of Wyoming, Colorado, Utah and Idaho unless otherwise noted.

- Wife's earning and personal property, not received from husband, in her sole control.

- Spouse's interest equal in each other's real estate.

- Equal pay for equal work, regardless of sex. Wyoming, Utah. (By custom in Colorado and Idaho)

- Professions and all public offices open to women.

- Jury service open to women. Utah, Idaho. (No prohibition in Wyoming and Colorado and women there act as jurors.)

- Equality in inheritance for both sexes.

- Divorce for same causes to husband and to wife, though wife can also secure separate maintenance of divorce for non-support.

- Wife and minor children entitled to homestead and to a certain allowance out of husband's estate, which has priority over ordinary debts.

- Women privileged to make a will at eighteen years of age.

- Free schools from primary grade through State University open to women.

- Free textbooks in public schools. Wyoming, Utah. (If district so vote in Colorado and Idaho.)

- Free kindergartens.

- American flag on schoolhouses.

- Compulsory education for children under sixteen years of age, with instruction in physiology and hygiene. Wyoming, Utah (Colorado, Idaho, under 14).

- Alcoholic drinks forbidden to minors.

- Tobacco forbidden to children under eighteen. Wyoming, Utah (Idaho, twenty-one, Colorado, sixteen).

- No children under fourteen to work in mines.

- No women to work in mines. Wyoming, Colorado, Utah. (Not customary in Idaho). Eight hour work maximum labor day for women. Colorado, Idaho.

- No factory work for children under fourteen. Colorado, Idaho. (Practically some in Utah and Wyoming.)

- Dependent children in family homes.

- Juvenile Courts and probation officers for delinquent children. Colorado, Utah, Idaho.

- Women physicians or matrons in certain institutions having women or children in custody. Wyoming, Colorado. (Customary in Utah and Idaho).

- Indecent exhibitions, pictures, or exposure and the sale or gifts of indecent literature forbidden.

- Gambling and prostitution forbidden.

- Age of consent eighteen or twenty-one years.

- Prostitutes and other lewd persons forbidden to register or vote. Idaho.

- Father and mother share in guardianship of children. Survivor the sole guardian.

Comments from the author:

These laws, with the exceptions noted, prevail in Wyoming, Colorado, Utah and Idaho where women vote on the same terms as men. I challenge the discovery of four man-suffrage States or Countries where women and children are equally protected.

May 25, 1908
Catharine Waugh McCulloch

Catherine Waugh McCulloch (1865 -1945) was a lawyer and noted suffragist (Wikipedia, "Catharine Waugh McCulloch"). A pioneer for women in the legal profession, she served as legal advisor (1904-1911) and vice-president (1910-1911) for the NAWSA.

Cartoons

Also in the Coggeshall collection in the Schlesinger Library, Radcliffe Institute, Harvard University are two cartoons, one in Boston, MA and one in Iowa.

This cartoon by J. N. Darling appeared in the Des Moines Register February 20, 1909, while the Iowa General Assembly was in session.

John Milton Coggeshall and Family

John Milton Coggeshall (JMC) was born into an Orthodox Quaker family at Back Creek, North Carolina on October 6, 1829 (Sample, 1986). Back Creek was (and still is) in western Randolph County. He must have been a small boy (five as reported in Haase, 2016) when the family moved to Indiana as his parents (Tristam and Milicent Coggeshall) were members of the Duck Creek Monthly Meeting in Henry County in June, 1833. When a new Monthly Meeting called Walnut Ridge was established in Rush County near Carthage, JMC and his parents joined and were charter members. They probably never lived in Henry County. Walnut Ridge was set off from Duck Creek in 1836 (Hamm, 9/3/2016). Henry and Rush Counties are near Fayette and Wayne Counties where the Whiteley and Ferris families settled.

The reasons for the Coggeshall move from North Carolina to Indiana in 1833 were quite similar to why Isaac Whiteley and his family left Maryland for Indiana in 1828. As stated by Lydia Whiteley Ferris in her genealogy, "Quakers were bitterly opposed to slavery and did not want to raise their families in slave states."

John transferred his Quaker membership to the Orthodox Milford Meeting just north of Milton in Wayne County (Sample, 1986). Because John Coggeshall and Mary Jane Whiteley were both disowned after marrying on November 10, 1857 outside of their faith, we were not sure where they were married. The two Friends meeting facilities in Milton were not available.

Professor Thomas Hamm, historian at Earlham College, which was founded by Quakers, established that they were married in Fayette County by W.J. Wallace, Mayor (Hamm, 07/27/2016) (Hamm, 9/4/2016). This suggests that they were married in Connersville, the county seat. He also added that they had a son named Abe when living in Washington Township in 1860, which would have been Wayne County and likely in Milton. Mary Catherine Sample did not mention an Abe in her listing of six Coggeshall children. Neither did Lydia Whiteley Ferris who confirmed Sample's data (Ferris, Lydia Whiteley, 1895). Since their first child in Sample's Whiteley genealogy was Olan T., born on March 23, 1863, a hiatus of five years between marriage and the first child in that era would be termed unusual.

Except for the first child, Mary Catherine Sample, a granddaughter of Daniel Whiteley, a brother of Issac, who poured over very extensive Quaker meeting records, has the following on children 2 to 7 of John and Mary Jane's seven children:

1. Abe was likely born in April, 1860. In the U.S. Census of June 1, 1860, he was listed as about one month old. He must have died early as there is no mention of him later. His existence was confirmed by Mary Jane Whiteley Coggeshall as she reported to the Census taker in 1900 that she was the mother of seven children, three living.

2. Olan T. was born in Milton, IN, March 23, 1863 and died on August 24, 1872, age 9 years.

3. Anna was born on January 25, 1865 and died 15 days later on February 9, 1865.

4. George Whiteley was born on December 21, 1867. (Author's note: Jake has the original card George sent to his aunt Lydia from Prescott Hall at Harvard in Cambridge, MA and a letter to his cousin Charles (Jake's grandfather) on the death of George's aunt Lydia.) On September 6, 1900, he married Anna Torrey in Beverly, MA and set up housekeeping in Dedham, MA.

5. Carl Carlton was born on August 26, 1872 and drowned on July 13, 1890, aged 18 years.

6. Harry Haden was born on April 7, 1876. He died in 1958 at the age of 82 (Haase, 2016).

7. Corrine was born on January 16, 1880 and married Ed Lingenfelter.

Olan T. likely traveled with his parents to Des Moines dying seven years later. Abe and Anna were likely buried in the Orthodox Friends cemetery in Milton, IN. The other four children were born in Des Moines. The period from late 1889 to mid 1890 must have been especially difficult for Mary Jane having lost her husband on November 27, 1889, at age 60, and son Carl on July 13, 1890, at age 18.

The Civil War and Quakers

Because of the peace testimony of the Quakers, the Civil War was a difficult test. So anti-slavery, why would they not join the military ranks to end it? Many did but to a less degree than others. According to a tabulation in a book by Nelson, "Sixty-two percent of all Indiana males between the ages of fifteen and forty-nine bore arms in the Civil War. Documented cases indicate that at least 21 percent of Quaker men enrolled. However, the percentage could be as much as 45 if undocumented cases were included (Nelson, 1991, p. 96)

While we do not know why the Coggeshalls left Milton for Des Moines in 1865, a judgement against John Milton appeared in the Milford (Orthodox) Meeting minutes in the first half of 1865. Quakers have been very attentive to members departing from unity for such things as lack of attendance and punctuality at meetings, excessive drinking, smoking, swearing, marrying contrary to the discipline, fornication, etc. When Jake ran across the resolution to JMC's problem in a random scanning of the minutes, he wondered, "What did he do?" Following is a transcription of the procedure from the men's minutes, typical of how they handled these issues (U.S. Quaker Meeting Records, 1681-1935, *Ancestry*).

(February 1865) "Milford Preparatory Meeting informs that John Milton Coggeshall has so far deviated from the order of the Society of Friends as to employ a substitute to do military service. Mordicai Hiatt and Robert S. Pritlow are appointed to treat with him on account thereof and report their sense of the disposition of his mind to the next -meeting."

(March 1865) "The Friends appointed to treat with John Milton Coggeshall report that they have had an opportunity with him and he did not appear prepared to condemn his misconduct. After a time of deliberating, the meeting unites in continuing the case of the same friend and they are directed to report to the next meeting."

(April 1865) "The committee continued in the case of John Milton Coggeshall reports they have had another interview with him and he having forwarded to the meeting an acknowledgement of his offense and request to be continued as a member accordingly. David Sutton and Jonathan Morris are appointed of the judgement of the meeting in the case and report to the next meeting."

(May 1865) "The committee to inform John Milton Coggeshall of the judgement of the meeting in his case report it has been attended to."

William Ferris, Coggeshall's brother-in-law was similarly charged in the Milford Hicksite branch in 1864. Quakers drafted into the Union Army in the Civil War could ask for exemption on conscientious grounds. Should he be arrested and sent to military prison, he should submit to all suffering in a manner representative of the Society of Friend's peaceable principles (Nelson, 1991). Conscientious objectors as well a non pacifists could avoid military service by hiring a substitute, as Coggeshall did, by paying an exemption fee of $300 or by performing an alternative service. Ferris elected to pay the $300 exemption fee which would be about $4000 in 2016 dollars.

Of note is that William Ferris was listed in the Nelson book but John Milton Coggeshall was not. However, of interest is that a Peter Coggeshall, son of Gayer and Hannah Coggeshall, paid the exemption fee as a member of the Milford Orthodox meeting. Two other Coggeshall sons of two different families in the New Garden meeting in Wayne County did serve in the military.

Nelson tabulated a total of 1,212 Quakers who faced conscription in the Civil War. Of that total, 148 were disowned, 220 produced offerings, 608 were not disciplined and 238 died (Nelson, 1991, p. 105).

The Coggeshalls in Des Moines, Iowa

(Author's note: Ann Delong Haase, Cynde's first cousin and also a great granddaughter of M.J. Coggeshall shared her recent Coggeshall genealogy which established the occupation of John Coggeshall. She also mentioned that the Coggeshalls frequently hosted many of the great suffragettes including Susan B. Anthony, Elizabeth Cady Stanton and Carrie Chapman Catt.)

As can be inferred from the activities and travels of Mary Jane, the Coggeshalls were a family of means. Notice the frequency of travel to the national and state suffrage conventions and invitations to Des Moines suffrage workers to "dine with me at my ?? restaurant." Very little has been known about the source of the Coggeshall wealth until Ann Delong Haase, first cousin of Cynde Coggeshall Fanter and great granddaughter of Mary Jane, furnished Cynde new information about the Coggeshall family (Haase, 2016).

We have no definitive reasons why the Coggshalls moved by covered wagon from Milton, IN to Des Moines, IA in 1865 but it might have been a business connection. Educated in the "common" schools, he learned the saddler's trade in Milton (The History of Des Moines and Polk County, 1911).

By the time the Coggeshalls left Milton, it was a thriving business community. By 1874, two railroads spanned the town. Industries included a manufacturer of farm implements, four lumber mills and two manufacturers of boots and shoes plus all the secondary and tertiary business connected to the basic industries (Ferris, John, 2010). John Coggeshall would have had an opportunity there to hone business skills.

According to *The History of Des Moines and Polk County*, John Coggshall never did follow his trade, as his inclination and talents attracted him in other directions. Here is a quotation from that book:

"Shortly after the close of the Civil War he came to Des Moines with Joseph Schlissler and William Jones, the three associating in the management of a clothing store on Third Street. Subsequently Mr. Coggeshall and Mr. Schissler engaged as partners in the same line of business, the relationship continuing for several years. Mr. Coggeshall, however, became interested in the manufacture of pottery and established a business of this nature in Des Moines, which, under his capable management, became highly lucrative.

(Author's note: Jake thoroughly searched on *Ancestry* both Joseph Schlisser and William Jones. Thinking that they might be connected as Quakers and living in Indiana before Des Moines. Nothing turned up on Schlissler but William W. Jones was born in Jefferson County, Indiana on February 21, 1815 and in the 1850 U.S. Census was residing in Des Moines, IA, fifteen years before the Coggeshalls moved there. In the 1880 U.S. Census, he was listed as a "Real Estate Dealer.")

As the years passed Coggeshall invested extensively in real estate and during the latter part of his life devoted his attention largely to his real-estate interests. He was also identified with various business concerns, serving as vice president of the State Insurance Company and adjuster for the Iowa Loan and Trust Company. He was interested with F.M Hubbell in securing the right of way of the Wabash Railroad in this city. His interest in Des Moines was shown while a member of the city council, in which he served for a number of years. He was chairman of the streets, alleys and bridges committee and was instrumental in securing many improvements that have assisted in giving to the city its present attractive appearance. In his business affairs he was remarkably successful, displaying a sound judgement which produced highly gratifying returns. He was energetic, reliable and progressive, and his public spirit contributed very greatly to the up building of the city."

We have few pictures of John and Mary Jane. Following is the only picture of them together found in a search for John Milton Coggeshall in *Ancestry*. This clearly shows that Mary Jane is over six years younger than John Milton.

Fig. 7 John Milton Coggeshall, who grew up near Milton, IN as did Mary Jane, became a very successful businessman in Des Moines, IA which supported Mary Jane's suffrage efforts in Iowa and nationally, from coast to coast. (Source: State Historical Society of Iowa, Des Moines)

Fig. 8 Separate photographs of John Milton and Mary Jane Coggeshall. Below is a picture post card with a line-up of unknown women except the elderly lady whose daughter, Corrine, penned, "My mother is in front of me (as she should be!)" (Source: Schlesinger Library)

As evidence of the wealth of the Coggeshall family is their home in Des Moines, IA. This picture post card is an example of the memorabilia saved for later generations by Jake's great grandmother, Lydia Whiteley Ferris.

Fig 9. The Coggeshall home at 210 Sixth Street in Des Moines, IA. (Source: Lydia Whiteley Ferris)

While this book is about Mary Jane Whiteley Coggeshall, we have to credit her husband who was able to support her suffrage movement in a very major way. These two Quakers from little Milton in east central Indiana became big, in a sense, on the Iowa and national suffrage stages.

Hicksite Quakers, the Heritage
of Mary Jane Whiteley Coggeshall

(Author's note: Jake's father was from a Hicksite Quaker family in Milton, Indiana and his mother was from an Orthodox Quaker family who originally settled in Milton. Two meetings existed for more than 50 years. The marriage in 1921 was in Jake's mother's home in Dublin, Indiana. At that time the only Quaker meeting in southwest Wayne County was the Orthodox meeting in Dublin, a community close to Milton. The split occurred at the same time that the Ferrises left the Wilmington, Delaware area for Milton. Jake's mother's grandfather came from North Carolina around 1836 to the Orthodox Milford Meeting just north of Milton. Her great great grandfather, John Bell, is credited with laying out Milton in 1824, and is buried in the Orthodox cemetery.)

Quakers, known for their peaceful ways, were also strong in opposition to slavery and strong in support of women and education. Robert Barclay wrote the premier theological work of early Friends, called *Apology for the True Christian Divinity* commonly known today simply as *Barclay's Apology* (Samuel, 1998). The *Apology* has fifteen propositions. A key statement in the Third Proposition concerns the scriptures which he describes as "a declaration of the fountain, and not the fountain itself, therefore they are not to be esteemed the principal ground of all truth and knowledge, nor yet the adequate primary rule of faith and manners. This points to the "Inner Light" which has been at the core of Quakerism over the years. Other propositions challenge the sacraments of baptism and communion.

Early Ferris Conversion to Quakers

David Ferris, brother to Jake's ancestor John back seven generations, was in a divinity school in Connecticut to become a Presbyterian minister in about 1730. In a Quaker meeting on Long Island, he heard several eminent ministers from Europe, both male and female. As he mentioned in his memoirs, "I heard women preach the gospel, in the divine authority of Truth; far exceeding all the learned rabbis I had known" (Ferris, David, 1779). Endowed by the "Inner Light," he dropped out of the divinity school and converted brothers Benjamin, John (Jake's ancestor), Zachariah and sister Hannah to Quakerism. David and his siblings including Hannah became ministers. The role of these ministers was to promote the faith, but they were not involved in the unprogrammed worship service.

The entrance of Hannah Ferris into Quaker ministry also reflects the importance that this society held for women and their role outside the home. A woman minister was unusual at this time and in this place. Her brother Benjamin stated in his journal, "The Presbyterians believed it to be heresy for a woman to preach to a congregation of people; not knowing, or not considering that both under the Law and under Gospel, women, as well as men had the gift of preaching and prophesying..." (Ferris, Benjamin). In the book, *History of the Towns of New Milford and Bridgewater, Connecticut, 1703-1882*, Samuel Orcutt, stated, in reference to Hannah, "This woman is reported to have been quite an efficient, successful preacher" (Orcutt, 1882).

Ancestor John married Abigail Tyron on March 15, 1738 in New Milford, CT in the home of his brother Joseph but connected to the Mamaroneck, NY meeting. Quaker weddings in homes were not uncommon. While not in a home, the format is described in the account of the church wedding of Lydia Whiteley, Mary Jane's sister, to William Ferris, in the Milford Hicksite meeting on pages 122 to 125. There were no ministers. The couple exchanged vows before witnesses and signed the document. Then the witnesses also signed the certificate confirming the union. The following picture illustrates what a Quaker home ceremony might have looked like.

Fig. 10 Often, Quaker weddings were held in homes. There was no minister. The couple took their vows before their members who signed their wedding document. (Source: Unknown.)

George Fox, the founder of the Society of Friends in the mid 1600s in England set the standard for the role of women. He established meetings of women. According to Barry Levy, "The responsibility of such women's meetings included visiting the sick, caring for young orphans, caring for poor Friends, disciplining younger women, inspecting the characters of women who announced their intention to marry, and overseeing all aspects of life which men or mixed company could not decently observe or discuss.....Fox effected his most radical fateful accomplishment in reorganizing the Anglo-American family; the encouragement and empowerment of spiritualized mothers as institutionalized in holy women's meetings" (Levy, 1988).

Leonard S. Kenworthy devoted an entire chapter in his 1981 book on *Quakerism* on the topic, "The Unique Role of Women in Quakerism." Examples are cited in this book supporting his examples of the early founding of co-educational colleges in the nineteenth century (Kenworthy, 1981). Other than Earlham, he cited Swarthmore, Guilford, and Whittier (later called George Fox College). While Haverford was not coeducational, Bryn Mawr, a women's college, was close by. Also mentioned was that many of the professors in those institutions were Quaker women.

Earlham, in Richmond, IN, was founded by the Society of Friends in 1847 as a boarding high school for the religious education of Quaker adolescents (Wikipedia, "Earlham College"). In 1859, it became Earlham College, a private, liberal arts institution. Richmond, the headquarters of Wayne County, is on the east side of the county with Milton on the southwest corner. Of note is that Earlham was the second U.S. institution of higher education to be coeducational. (Author's note: This is an area for further research. In any case, Earlham College was early.)

Kenworthy cites Margaret Bacon in her book on the prominence of Quaker women including that of the first eight women doctors in the United States, five were Quakers (Bacon, 1974). Kenworthy continued with, "Following the Civil War and the Emancipation Proclamation, American Quakers saw an opportunity to assist Negroes (the term used in those days) to assist in a variety of ways, especially in helping them to obtain a basic education. Thus, young Quaker women from the north went south to start schools. For Quaker young people that was the equivalent in those times of the recent Peace Corps."

One of these young "Peace Corps" type women was Anna Stanton, first cousin of Mary Jane Whiteley Coggeshall and Lydia Whiteley Ferris. For this reason, her career as a teacher in home economics is included in this section.

The Hicksite Split

In 1828, there was a major separation in the Quakers, led by Elias Hicks. The Hicksites clung more to tradition while the Orthodox were moving in the direction of other protestant churches where the Bible was more central to their faith than the individual. Following on the next page is the top of the first page of men's meeting minutes of the Milford Hicksite branch declaring the split.

The key to the Hicksite Quaker faith is the beauty of silence and the "Inner Light." Hicks considered the Inner Light as the primary authority and all external aids even the Scriptures as secondary. If he had a favorite text it was either the twenty seventh verse of the first chapter of Colossians: "Christ in you, the hope of glory" or the ninth verse of the first chapter of John: "the true light which lighteth every man that cometh into the world" (Forbush 1956, p. 194). He realized that the Bible contained many contradictions and inconsistencies and believed that it was written by fallible men. The Hicksite Quakers, as did the Orthodox, did not believe in water baptism and communion. Also, Hicks did not believe that it was vital for Quakers to believe in the miracles of the Bible.

Lucretia Coffin Mott was inspired by minister Elias Hicks (Wikipedia, "Lucretia Mott"). That Lucretia Coffin Mott, Susan B. Anthony and Mary Jane Whiteley Coggeshall were all three Hicksite Quakers is remarkable and, deserving further analysis, is the reason for this extended coverage. This adds credibility to the observation that, "With the Hicksite-Orthodox split of 1827-1828, Orthodox women found their spiritual role decreased, while Hicksite women retained greater influence" (Wikipedia, "Quakers").

(Author's note: While not raised in the Hicksite branch of the Society of Friends, Jake did experience their unprogrammed worship service in Newcastle-upon-Tyne in 1969-70 when on a project with Michigan State University. His wife and two small children were with him. While often called a silent meeting, it was not. Those in attendance broke the silence by their observations about their lives and experiences linked to their faith. Seats were arranged on four sides of a table which included a Bible and a vase of flowers. There was no minister, no music and no rose windows. Behind one window was a garden; behind another, a brick wall. The meeting adjourned when the clerk turned and shook hands with the nearby person. While we missed the music, we found the service strengthened our faith and provided interaction with the Quaker community.)

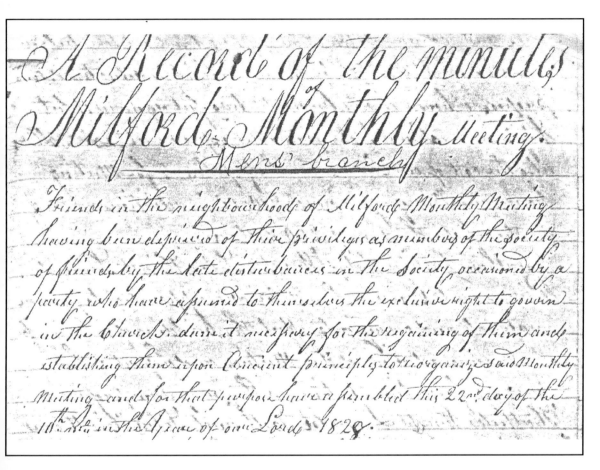

Fig. 11 Top of the first page of the Milford Hicksite men's monthly meeting in 1828 in Milton, IN announcing the separation from the Orthodox group. (Source: Watson Library, Wilmington College, Wilmington, OH).

Anna M. Stanton, first cousin of M. J. Coggeshall & Lydia Whiteley Ferris

Another remarkable woman with a Whiteley/Ferris connection was Anna M. Stanton, a first cousin of Mary Jane and Lydia's and also a Hicksite Quaker. A single woman, born in Milton, IN, she became a teacher of home economics and traveled extensively from the Midwest to the Atlantic coast and back. Her father died when she was five years of age making her achievements especially noteworthy. Her relatives and friends coaxed her into writing her autobiography (Stanton, 1908). It has been a valuable source for purposes of history and genealogical research. It was published in Des Moines, IA in 1908, a busy year for Mary Jane Whiteley Coggeshall. We can speculate that Anna was visiting as she did often with her first cousins.

Her life was fascinating in that she lived in so many homes either as a boarder or a guest. Sounding like "Little House on the Prairie," she told about her housing while teaching in a new settlement on the bleak prairie in extreme northwest Iowa in 1868. As she described her living quarters, "Two brothers had taken up a claim and put up a house of hewn logs, every log brought thirty miles by an ox team. The size of the house was 16x18, all one room. The single brother had his bed on his side of the house, the married brother on his side. For me a cot was made and it was so near the cook stove I could put my hand on it. It took a good deal of maneuvering to get in and out of bed. Fortunately, the young man was not there much of the time. They were good pure minded people and I got along very well, but to those used to their own private room it was a little hard to reconcile."

In February, 1870, Anna received a call to teach at a freedman's school in Mt. Pleasant, South Carolina very close to Charleston. She was urged to come immediately, and the directors of the school found a young man to finish her unexpired term. This school for African Americans was founded by Cornelia Hancock, a noted volunteer nurse for the Union Army during the Civil War (Wikipedia, "Cornelia Hancock"). Hancock was born in Hancocks Bridge, New Jersey in 1840 "to Quakers of old colonial ancestry" and died in 1927. She was a Hicksite.

When the school closed for the summer about the first of June, 1870, most of the teachers headed north. Having only arrived in March, Anna elected to stay and occupy the boys with basket making of palmetto and long grass; the girls sewed and braided palmetto for hats. Yellow fever broke out in Charleston, and the demand for houses including the lighthouse island where the teachers stayed allowed them to buy a cottage on Sullivan's Island where it would be more healthy. She did survive when acquaintances did not.

But the respect that Anna commanded in her short tenure there was expressed by this quotation, "I felt a fear I might take it and spread it over the village. But some of my good, true colored friends came to me and said, 'This is your home, Miss Stanton, stay right here. If you get sick you shall have the best care we can give you. Your friends are here. We could not go to the island and you would fall into the hands of strangers.' This was Rebecca Jackson and her sister, whom I have had more than one occasion to remember."

After then, Anna did return to the north during the summers. She remained at the school for 10 years when she became involved in another similar school for African Americans in Virginia. She had a class of girls and taught them to sew, cut and make garments and gave special lessons in making button holes, repairing garments, knitting, etc.

Having worked with African Americans extensively, Anna remarked, "I have often been asked my opinion on the negro problem. As I have had some years' experience with them, I would say we find much the same characteristics we see in the white race. The color seems only the outward coating. I have spent nearly twenty years of my life with them. I have found in them the genuine friendship, and in some true appreciation of the labor put forth for their elevation."

"The children, like all others, vary in degree of faculty. Some are slow, others quick. The work in which I felt the greatest interest was in teaching them to make pleasant, healthy homes. In this respect there is a great reformation needed. And the hope is in the children. Every teacher should endeavor to instill this into their lives by example as well as precept."

Anna Stanton and her friend Cornelia Hancock are additional examples of the Hicksite Quaker heritage as it relates to the early role of women in leadership positions and concerns about social justice. In addition, while Quaker men bought themselves out of serving in the Civil War, their families harbored slaves in the Under Ground Railroad throughout the North and including eastern Indiana (Dobson, 2009).

Anna Stanton and cousin Mary

Anna Stanton, as clearly indicated in her autobiography, kept a detailed diary on years, places and people. As a single person, she embraced many families and in particular those of Mary Jane Whitely Coggeshall and Lydia Whiteley Ferris. Since Anna was born in Milton in 1832, she would have known Lydia, also born in 1832 and Mary Jane, born in 1836, as children. One of her visits to Des Moines was preceded by teaching in Milton. To share this relationship over time through 1907 in Anna's own words, following are extractions from her book:

"In 1864, I was visiting in Milton, and decided to teach a subscription school, and had the Friends meeting house offered me. I opened, had a pretty good attendance for a few days, then they fell off. I wished for a reason for it. I had admitted two black sheep into the flock; some objected to sending their children. I told them I was sorry to lose them, but could not go back on my promise to the colored mother, a poor but respectable washerwoman in the place. I kept right on with the few that came. I think I boarded at Uncle Isaac Wright's. Some of my friends stood by me and said they were glad of the stand that I had taken. Samuel Morris said to me one day at meeting, 'I am so glad, that here is five dollars to help thee out.' Cousin Isaac Whiteley, Sr. (Mary Jane's father), said, 'I also want to help thee with five.'" (Author's note: Five dollars in 1864 would be about sixty-five 2016 dollars.)

(Forward to the fall of 1868) "I taught after this in different places and in the fall of 1868 I went to Des Moines, Iowa, to visit relatives I had not seen for some years. John Milton Coggeshall and family were living there, with whom I had a pleasant visit. They had two little boys, the oldest in school. We had a very pleasant visit together."

(Forward to 1891) "After visiting a friend in Chicago, I decided to make a visit to Des Moines, as I had not visited my cousin there for some years. This cousin had lost her husband and one son not long before (husband John on November 27, 1889 and son Carl on July 13, 1890). I also went to LeMars (where Anna lived in the "Little House on the Prairie" in 1868) to visit my sister's family. There I found changes in family and surroundings. It seemed now a country of timber. The dear sister had been called away, the family married and scattered, and one daughter a widow.

After a good visit I returned to Des Moines to spend the winter at my cousin's, as she wished it. She had two sons and a daughter, one son in Harvard College, the other son and the daughter in school here. In this pleasant home I remained for over five years, with little to do. I felt sometimes that I must do something, if it was only to bake a kind of gingersnap that some of my friends liked very much." (Author's note: Mary Jane had help in "my restaurant.")

(Forward to August – September 1900) "I was to go to Boston to meet my cousins from Des Moines, Iowa, the Coggeshalls, who were to spend two weeks in the vicinity of Boston, Mass., and attend the wedding of George, Cousin Mary's eldest son.

Cousin Corinne (Mary Jane's daughter) met me at the station and we went to their boarding place, the Arlington. It was a hot day. As we were not far from the 'Common,' we walked through the Public Garden, over to the Shaw Memorial, then to the Woman's Journal office and saw Mr. Blackwell (Henry Blackwell, the husband of Lucy Stone who died in 1893).

Tuesday, August 28. Corinne and I went out to do some shopping. After we returned Mr. and Miss Blackwell (Henry Blackwell and Alice Stone Blackwell) called to see cousin Mary, and that afternoon we all went to Beverly to take up our abode there for some days. Harry (Mary Jane's son) had secured rooms for us on Lathrop Street, the house near the water.

September 4. We went into Boston. I bought some little sherbet glasses to give to the bride and groom. We went in the evening to Dr. Torrey's to see the wedding presents, which were very numerous and very elegant.

September 6 was the eventful day long looked forward to. At 4 p.m. the company met in Dr. Torrey's parlor, and oh! It was so hot. After the ceremony and congratulations were over, refreshments were passed, and then the bride and groom slipped off, as they thought slyly; but a shower of rice and some old shoes followed them, and also some other marks of the married couple."

(Forward to 1907 when she returned to Des Moines) "The State Suffrage convention met while I was there, my cousin entertaining some of the delegates. Mrs. Coggeshall also made a dinner one evening, and invited retiring officers."

The Whiteley-Ferris Connection

Mary Catherine Sample's book on *The Whiteley Family* has no record of their freeing slaves, but their religious ties to a denomination called Nicholites would indicate that they might have because of their opposition to slavery. Jake's ancestor, Nathan Ferris, back six generations manumitted 10 slaves on a farm on the Eastern Shore of Maryland in 1782. The manumission document stated in part, "Know all men by these presents that I Nathan Ferris of Caroline County Maryland being in possession of ten Negroes, viz. Lydia, Esther, Solomon, Rachael, Betty, George, James, Israel, Job and Grace and being satisfied that they have an indisputable right in equity to enjoy their freedom when of proper age hereby manumit and declare the said ten persons free as they severally arrive at the day and time herein after affixed …" (Maryland State Archives).

The Ferris and Whiteley families were well acquainted before leaving Quaker settlements on the Eastern Shore of Maryland in the first part of the 1800s. The Whiteleys converted to Quakers from a society known as "Nicholites" about the time that Mary Jane's father, Isaac, was born. For 40 years, the Nicholites worshipped separately, but by the beginning of the nineteenth century they were absorbed by the Quakers. Their beliefs were close to those of the Quakers as documented in a set of ten "Queries" Jake discovered in the Friends Collection at Swarthmore College in Pennsylvania.

Remarkably, there is another Whiteley-Ferris tie. In 1847, Anthony Whiteley, Jr., uncle of Mary Jane Whiteley Coggeshall, sent a manuscript entitled, "Queries of the Nicholite Friends" to Benjamin Ferris, grandson of John, cited earlier of having been to converted to Quaker by brother David. Benjamin was noted as an historian and as a civic and religious leader in Wilmington, DE. He corresponded with Elias Hicks, who generated the split in the Friends Society. He was likely influential in convincing the Whiteley as well as the Ferris families to join the Hicksites. Anthony was a child when his family were Nicholites. Here is the letter from Anthony to Benjamin introducing the Queries:

> My esteemed Friend,
> A dear, but distant brother who (like myself) is of the Nicholite stock, has recently transmitted to me the queries that were used by that society. They were new to me, and I thought that they might be so to thee, if thou

hast not previously seen them. It was the first meeting for worship that I ever attended, and is cherished as among my earliest recollections. I often revert to it with feelings of pleasure, that I was introduced, at so tender age, into a religious meeting where unaffected piety was so amply manifested. On reading the third query, I felt a living desire that our third was in conformity with its simplicity.

Thy friend

3rd Month 13th 1847

1st   Are all Friends meetings, for worship and discipline duly and timely attended, and are Friends preserved from sleeping or needless going in and out of meeting, or any other uncomely behavior therein?

2nd Are Friends careful to avoid the occasion of any discord among them; and if any arise, is speedy endeavors used to end them; is talebearing, back biting and evil reports discouraged, and care taken not to speak that in absence of any that may tend only to expose them?

3rd Are Friends careful to bring up those who are under their immediate direction to the due attendance of meeting, to plainness of speech, behavior and apparel, and in frequent reading the Scriptures and other useful books, and restrain them from reading pernicious books; from frequenting the company of those that are of a disorderly behavior, and from the corrupt conversations of the world?

4th Are Friends careful to be at a word in all their traffic, and give good weight and measure, and avoid that evil practice of multiplying words to set their stuff to sale?

5th Are Friends careful to settle their accounts annually, or as often as need may require so as to give their creditors no cause to blame them; and careful in their engagements, and faithful to perform them? Are the necessities of the poor duly inspected and they assisted agreeably to their circumstances?

6th Are Friends careful in the use of spirituous liquors to only make the needful use of them, and when their business takes them out amongst other people are they careful to avoid light and needless discourse and not to be drawn away with the evil of the wicked?

7th Are Friends striving against the uncomely practice of laughter when speaking about religious matters?

8th Are Friends careful to keep from making or buying any dyes, stripes, flowers, corded or mined stuff, and from all needless cuts and fashions, and bear a faithful testimony against the pernicious sin of pride?

9th Are Friends careful to bear a faithful testimony against slavery in its various branches, and provide in a suitable manner for those in their families that have had their freedom secured to them, and they instructed to useful learning, and is the welfare of such as have been set free attended to, and the necessities of them relieved?

10th Is care taken to deal regular with offenders in the spirit of meekness and wisdom without partiality or unnecessary delay?

These queries are included and discussed in a book entitled *Joseph Nichols and the Nicholites* by Kenneth Carroll (Carroll, 1962). He also authored an excellent book for genealogists entitled, *Quakerism on the Eastern Shore* (Carroll, 1970).

John Ferris, Jake's ancestor back five generations, who was head of the family which migrated to Milton, actually moved from the Eastern Shore to a farm near Wilmington, DE in 1809, following his brother William. He became a cabinetmaker in addition to operating a 64 acre farm. That William and John were first cousins of the famous Benjamin Ferris along with other Ferrises in Wilmington may have been a factor in the move.

In any case, John Ferris, at age 55, with wife Anna (also formerly a Nicholite) and four children left the Wilmington area for the Milford Monthly Meeting in Milton of eastern Indiana in 1828. While absent from the Eastern Shore of Maryland for 19 years, we believe the Ferris-Whiteley tie continued.

Reasons for moving to Indiana may relate to the opening up of the frontier and the growing population of Quakers in the region. By tradition, as stated in a genealogy of the Whiteley family, "The two brothers, Isaac and Daniel Whiteley, together with some other friends, neighbors, associates and their families, who had espoused, or inclined to, the 'Quaker Faith,' and were bitterly opposed to slavery in any form, decided that they did not want to raise their families in Maryland, a slave state, and they emigrated with their families to Indiana in 1828" (Ferris, Lydia Whiteley, 1895).

We believe the Ferrises, though from Delaware, did travel with the Whiteleys. This linkage would have been quite convenient since the most likely route by covered wagon from Wilmington would have been through Baltimore where the Whiteleys and others from the Eastern Shore of Maryland would have joined with the Ferrises. Based on research by Elliott, the most likely route from Baltimore would have been the Cumberland Road to Cumberland, Maryland, then the National Road through Washington, Pennsylvania; Wheeling, West Virginia; Columbus, Ohio; and Richmond, Indiana; then to Milton, Indiana (Elliott, 1969).

This may have been confirmed by Anna Stanton in her autobiography (Stanton, 1908):

> Seven families came together when he (Isaac Whiteley) came, all in their covered wagons. He was very jovial and pleasant, and to prepare shelter for the women and children at night he went ahead and would try to engage rooms at some farm house for them to spread their beds upon the floor. But one evening when on the lookout for a stopping place, he saw a man sitting on a log, if I remember rightly, not far from a house. Cousin Isaac spoke to him and asked if they could secure lodging for the night for their women and children. The man asked how many. Cousin answered, "Seven wives and forty children." "Well," said the man, "on condition that there shall be no swearing, nor stealing." This, no doubt, offended Cousin Isaac's dignity to find there could be a doubt of their honesty, and he called back to the nearest team, "We will drive on." They afterwards learned that the man was a preacher.
>
> This company of settlers, they say, was seven weeks on their way, arriving at last, dusty, weary and foot sore, but glad of a resting place. I think our mothers must have been able to endure more than their daughters can in this day.

Anna Stanton went on to describe pioneer life in that section of the frontier:

> Those who found not a ready made home must make one, by cutting down trees and building a log cabin. Happy, indeed, when they had windows and doors tight enough to keep out the wolves and night intruders.

Isaac Whiteley lived west of Milton, which was in Wayne County, on a farm just over the line in Fayette County from the spring of 1829 to the summer of 1867 (Sample, 1986). Of course, his wife and family lived there for at least part of this period. On this property is a log cabin restored in 1977 by the Brower family as pictured below.

Fig. 12 This restored log cabin likely belonged to Isaac Whiteley or John Ferris after their settlement west of Milton, IN circa 1830.

Of particular interest is that the owner, Campbell Brower, notified Jake's family that in the restoration, "J. Ferris" was engraved in the plaster removed from the exterior with the date, "11/21/183?." One can speculate that either John Ferris or his son Joseph helped Isaac in constructing the log cabin. However, John and Levi Hopper bought 125 acres in or close to that site on May 27, 1830 and sold it on April 1, 1833 to Samuel Baldwin who sold the southeast corner of the property to Daniel Whiteley on June 6, 1833. Not clear is whether the log cabin belonged to Isaac Whiteley, John Ferris or Daniel Whiteley. John probably moved into the town of Milton in 1837, so it could have been his. In any case, the cabin represents the typical dwelling of the Ferrises and Whiteleys and establishes their continued close association.

The Milford Friends (Orthodox) established their meeting north of Milton in 1819, so the Quakers were active in the community nearly ten years before the Whiteleys and

Ferrises arrived. It is doubtful that either family attended that meeting. The Milford Friends (Hicksite) established their meeting on October 22, 1828 and in 1829 a frame building was constructed on the banks of the West Branch of the Whitewater River in Milton (Heiss, 1972).

The Orthodox meeting was laid down in 1882 as was the Hicksite meeting in 1911. So, in little Milton, two Quaker meetings were active for over 50 years, from 1829 to 1882. With Jake's father from the Hicksite line and his mother from the Orthodox line, this schism had closed by the time they were married in 1921. (Author's note: In Philadelphia in 2000, Jake detected some continuing demarcation.)

Following are pictures of the exterior and interior of the Hicksite meeting house before it was torn down, where William Ferris and Lydia Whiteley were married. On the exterior, note the two doors to provide separate seating for the men and women. On the interior note the plainness. The cushions on some of the benches were apparently the only luxury for the hour and a half unprogrammed services.

While the Hicksite meeting house was dismantled around 1911, remnants of the Orthodox meeting house, which was brick, remains and is part of a commercial operation. Both were next to the Whitewater Canal and their graveyards were next to the meetings.

Fig. 13 The exterior of the Milford Hicksite Meeting House in Milton, IN on the banks of the west branch of the Whitewater River, shuttered in 1911.

Fig. 14 The interior of the Milford Hicksite Meeting House in Milton, IN.

The William Ferris-Lydia Whiteley Wedding

The Hicksite Quakers were very careful in judging the behavior of their members including the suitability for couples who announced their intention to marry. Here is an extraction from the men's minutes relative to Jake's great grandfather William Ferris and great grandmother Lydia Whiteley:

> The committee appointed to make inquiry into William Ferris's clearness of other marriage engagements, report they find nothing to hinder his proceeding therin and Lydia Ann Whiteley, and continuing their intentions, are left at liberty to accomplish the said agreeably to our order. Daniel Reulon and Elias Moore are appointed to attend the marriage, see that it be orderly accomplished, place the certificate in the hands of the recorder, and report to the next meeting.

Just as there were no ministers in the Hicksite service, marriages were also conducted without preachers. Those present signed as witnesses. Following is the wording of the certificate for the wedding of William Ferris and Lydia Ann Whiteley, and a partial copy of the 45 signatures from the original document. On the right side of the lower section are the signatures of William and Lydia. Those below include Mary Jane Whiteley. On the left side of the lower section is the signature of J.M. Coggeshall. Apparently Mary Jane and JMC were not seated together -- typical for Quakers.

Whereas William Ferris of Milton, in the County of Wayne and State of Indiana, son of Joseph Ferris of the same place and Deborah his wife, and Lydia Ann Whiteley, daughter of Isaac Whiteley of the County of Fayette and State aforesaid, and Lydia A. his wife; having informed Milford monthly meeting of the religious society of Friends that they intend marriage with each other, and having consent of parents, their said proposals of marriage were allowed by said meeting. These are to certify whom it may concern, that for the accomplishment of their marriage, this twenty-fifth day of the tenth month, in the year of our Lord one thousand eight hundred and fifty-five, they, the said William Ferris and Lydia Ann Whiteley, appeared in a public meeting of said people, held at Milford aforesaid, and the said William Ferris taking the said Lydia Ann Whiteley by the hand declared that he took her, the said Lydia Ann Whiteley, to be his wife, promising, with divine assistance, to be unto her a loving and faithful husband, until death should separate them: — and then the said Lydia Ann Whiteley did in like manner declare that she took him, the said William Ferris, to be her husband, promising with divine assistance, to be unto him a loving and faithful wife, until death should separate them. And moreover, they, the said William Ferris and Lydia Ann Whiteley, (she, according to the custom of marriage, — adopting the name of her husband) did, as a further confirmation thereof, then and there, to these presents, set their hands.

And we whose names are also hereunto subscribed, being at the solemnization of said marriage, have, as witnesses thereto, set our hands, the day and year above written.

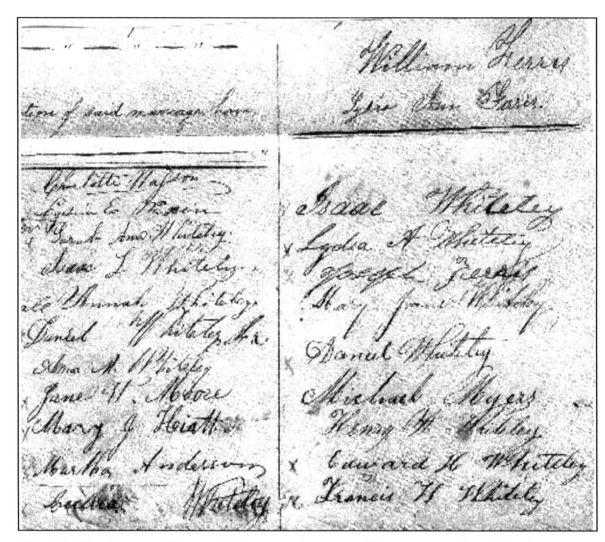

Fig. 15 The bottom lines of this marriage certificate state that "And we whose names are also hereunto subscribed, being at the solemnization of said marriage, have, as witnesses thereto, set our hands, the day and year above written. (Note Mary Jane Whiteley's signature.)

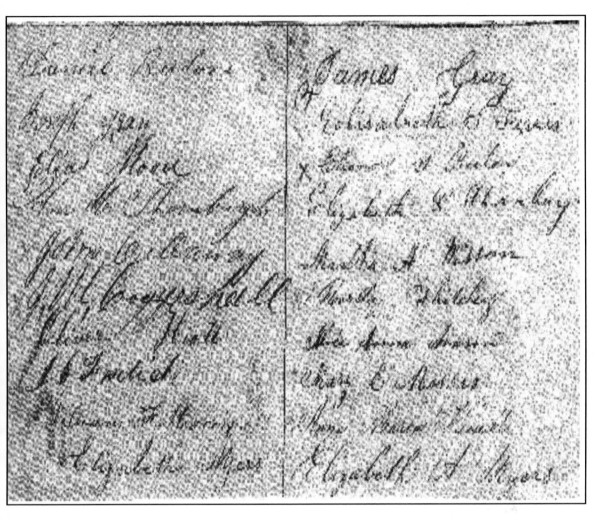

Fig. 16 Mary Jane Whiteley's signature was on the right side at the bottom of the wedding certificate. On the left side at the bottom was the prominent signature of J. M. Coggeshall. Of course, by Quaker tradition, they were seated on the opposite side of the Milford Hicksite Meeting House in Milton, IN.

Obituary and Poem in Memory of
Mary Jane Whiteley Coggeshall

(Author's note: Jake has an original copy of a page from a publication which is not from a newspaper but a magazine. The page contained an obituary of Mary Jane Whiteley Coggeshall and her picture. On the rest of the page are short articles and poems with a personal and rural flair. This must have been published soon after Mary Jane's passing in December 1911. Part of the last paragraph is missing as are the endings of lines of a poem dedicated to Mary Jane by Alice S. Longley.)

Obituary (Source: Not known)

In the passing of Mrs. Mary J. Coggeshall not Des Moines and Iowa alone, but the country at large, has suffered a great loss. Her influence had long ago extended beyond the limits of her own state. Her's was a great and true spirit, whose influence for good no mortal could measure. In Des Moines, her home town, where she had raised her children and where she was loved and honored by all who knew her, the mourning of her death was universal. As a splendid factor for progress her loss was deplored. As a sweet and loving mother none can replace her. As a genuine, inspiring friend, true and loyal in prosperity and in need, the world holds few who are her equal. To be capable of friendship – this is the highest praise. All other fine qualities are included in this. And her friends who loved her because of her friendship to them, are legion. I am one of those. Coming to Des Moines a young girl to teach in the high school, I was taken into her family as a member of it. I grew to love her and wonder at the splendor of the woman. She knew life in all its phases. She was highly intellectual and of an inquiring mind. She delved into the lore of past ages. She studied with discrimination the civic and social conditions of today. She loved a rare poem as a child loves the sunshine. She discussed a tremendous problem as unerringly as did Kant. All the while, she cared first of all things for the welfare and happiness of her husband and children. In the kitchen, in the sewing room, at her palette (she painted much in years gone by), on the veranda with her books, rocking her little girl to sleep in the dusk with other children drowsing about her, directing the councils of the political organizations to which

126

she belonged, writing a keen editorial for some journal, or entertaining distinguished guests in her parlors, she was always the same, always lovely, gracious and wonderful in her womanliness. One of her great characteristics was a fine appreciation of good qualities in others. She seldom blamed people, always was praising them. Love was the keynote of her being. In the midst of suffering, where one darling boy, just entering manhood, was brought home drowned, she said to a friend who was trying to help, "You don't know how much I love you for all you are doing for me!" Love was reflected in her high bred, beautiful face. This lovely face seemed to sadden as the years went by, as time after time she saw the failure of her dearest hope – the passage of the suffrage bill in Iowa.

That any real man with daughters, wife and mother of his own, could discuss this question with her, and refuse to vote for it, is one of the great mysteries. To have known her was a liberal education. Her example was a great one. Her person__ ……… so rare, that all who came ……… influence did her homage …….. spirit is like a star, shining ………. ever, shining for you, for the whole human race.

Poem (Source: Alice S. Longley)

All hail and farewell to Mary Jane Coggeshall,
To Mary so gracious, so …… so true.
A bright star was added to the Heavenly Kingdom,
Just as our old year was added to new.
We are lonely without you …….. for and miss you,
Your place among us to fill.
Your strength and your ……. Inspired us to action,
And that inspiration is with us still.
So softly and quiet the ……… took you,
And bore you away to ……… shore.
We are dazed, we are ……… onward as ever.
We will work 'till we meet you once more.
– Alice S. Longley

A Personal Tribute to Mary Jane Whiteley Coggeshall

When Jake started writing the "Genealogy of the Ferris Family of Milton, Indiana," in the 1970s, he was so impressed by the role played by Mary Jane Whiteley Coggeshall in the women's suffrage movement. From time to time he added to the genealogy and finally did complete it in 2010. In 2012, having learned that the Coggeshall archives were in the Schlesinger Library, at the Radcliffe Institute at Harvard University, he was able to obtain a CD of some 18 speeches and additional material. Nearly all of her speeches were in her handwriting, and in early 2016, he transcribed them into Microsoft Word. He did have one typewritten speech which had been in the possession of his great grandmother. In August 2016, he spent three days at the library and had access to archives not reviewed in his 2012 visit.

Jake does believe that her Hicksite Quaker faith inspired and enabled her to take up the challenge of the woman suffrage movement as such faith did Lucretia Coffin Mott, Susan B. Anthony and the Hicksite Quaker women in the vicinity of Seneca Falls, NY where the movement was born. This emanated from the Hicksite liberal interpretation of the Bible. As stated by Coggeshall in her 1893 speech before the Equality Club of Eagle Grove, IA, "Ninety nine pulpits out of every hundred have taught that women should not meddle in politics."

The Quakers in general, in comparison to other religious groups were very early to involve women and very early to condemn slavery. The Hicksite Quakers were not only leaders in the women's suffrage movement but were also active in the Underground Railroad and the education of blacks in the South following the Civil War. As commendable as these charitable acts were during the nineteenth century, membership did not grow even into the twentieth century; and the membership is quite small today. Unfortunately, they were not evangelical, their plain sanctuaries, strict rules of conduct, lack of music, and the unprogrammed service were turnoffs for many, and the Hicksite split was a deterrent.

Leonard Kenworthy concluded in his 1981 book on a slightly optimistic note, "Yes, the Religious Society of Friends is an infinitesimally small, fragile, fragmented group. But it has a remarkable message and a glorious history. Its future could be as great as its past. As we pray the prayer of Thomas Kelly: 'Open Thou my life. Guide my thoughts where I dare not let them go. But Thou darest. Thy will be done'" (Kenworthy, 1981).

Jake thanks God for the privilege and ability to research this remarkable woman and live long enough in retirement to honor her substantial contribution to humanity. After 41 years of a tremendous effort to get women in Iowa and nationally the right to vote, she passed away in 1911, nine years before the Nineteenth Amendment to the U.S. Constitution. In her memorial service tribute to Susan B. Anthony in 1906, she concluded with a quote from another, "She came into the world crying while all about her laughed – she left the world smiling while all about her wept."

Dear Mary Jane Whiteley Coggeshall, "Your great grand nephew is weeping."

Bibliography

Ancestry, an online family history resource, Ancestry.com.

Bacon, Margaret H., *The Quaker Struggle for the Rights of Women*, American Friends Service Committee, 1974.

Blackwell, Alice Stone, "Women's Edition of the Register and Leader," May 12, 1915, Des Moines, IA.

Carroll, Kenneth, *Joseph Nichols and the Nicholites*, Coyright by Kenneth Carroll, The Easton Publishing Company, Easton MD, 1962.

Carroll, Kenneth, *Quakerism on the Eastern Shore*, The Maryland Historical Society, Copyright by the Maryland Historical Society, Library of Congress Catalogue Card No. 70-112986, Garamond/Pridemark Press, Baltimore, MD, 1970.

Caswell, Suzanne, "Celebrate Woman Suffrage," *Trail Tales, The Journal of Boone County History*, Summer/Fall 2008, No. 110, Boone County Historical Society, Boone Iowa.

Coggeshall, Charles Pierce and Thellwell Russell, *The Coggeshalls in America*, C.E Goodspeed and Company, Boston, MA, 1930.

Dobson, Melonie, *Love Finds You in Liberty, Indiana*, 2009, Summerside Press, Inc.,11024 Quebec Circle, Bloomington, Minnesota 55438, www.summerside.com

Elliott, Errol T., *Quakers on the American Frontier*, The Friends United Press, Richmond, IN, 1969.

Fanter, Cynde Coggeshall, Personal communication, April 2, 2002.

Fanter, Cynde Coggeshall, Personal communications, 2016.

Fanter, Cynde Coggeshall, "Quiet and Not so Quiet," a "Proteus" paper. Proteus is a club in Des Moines founded in 1896 by Della Marquardt Coggeshall, daughter-in-law of Mary Jane's. This excellent paper focused on the Woman Suffrage Movement with some additional information on the career of Mary Jane Coggeshall, (February 6, 2012).

Ferris, Benjamin, "Journal," Benjamin Ferris of Oblong, NY (1708-1775), Ferris Collection, Friends Historical Library, Swarthmore College, PA.

Ferris, David, *Memoirs of the Life of David Ferris*, The first version was completed in May 1779 and in 1855 published by the Merrihew and Thompson's Steam Power Press, Merchant Street above Fourth, Philadelphia.

Ferris, John N., "Genealogy of the Ferris Family of Milton, Indiana," 2010.

Ferris, Lydia Ann Whiteley, "Genealogy of the Whiteley Familly," 1895.

Forbush, Bliss, *Elias Hicks, Quaker Liberal*, Columbia University Press, New York, 1956.

Gordon, Eleanor Elizabeth, "Suffrage Parade – Boone Iowa," *Trail Tales*, The Journal of Boone County History, Summer/Fall 2008, No. 110, Boone County Historical Society, Boone Iowa.

Haase, Ann Delong, unpublished genealogy of the Coggeshall family, 2016.

Hamm, Thomas, an email on July 27, 2016.

Hamm, Thomas, an email on July 28, 2016.

Hamm, Thomas, an email on September 4, 2016.

Heiss, Williard, *Abstracts of the Records of the Society of Friends of Indiana, Part 4, Encyclopedia of American Quaker Genealogy*, Vol. VII, Indiana Historical Society, Indianapolis, 1972.

Kenworthy, Leonard S., *Quakerism, A Study Guide on the Religious Society of Friends*, printed by the Print Press, Dublin, IN, 1981.

Levy, Barry, *Quakers and the American Family, British Settlement in the Delaware Valley*, Oxford University Press, 1988.

Maryland State Archives, Caroline County Court (Land Records), MSA C523, Nathan Ferris, folio 579-580, 1771-1786. Dates: 1779-1786. Description: A, pp 451-900, iPhotostatic Copy Accession No.: 10,099-2. [MSA No.:C523-2. Location: 1/2/1/2], Annapolis, MD.

Mills, Elizabeth Ferris, "Autobiography on nine handwritten pages," circa 1947.

Nelson, Jacquelyn S., *Indiana Quakers Confront the Civil War*, Indiana Historical Society, 1991.

Orcutt, Samuel, *History of the Towns of New Milford and Bridgewater, Connecticut, 1703-1882*, Press of the Case, Lockwood and Brainard Company, 1882.

Sample, Mary Catherine Templin, *The Whiteley Family,* Volume 1, April, 1986.

Samuel, Bill, "Friends (Quakers) and the Bible,"
http://www.suite101.com/linkcategory.cfm/1370/8175

Schlesinger Library, Radcliffe Institute, Harvard University, Papers of Mary Jane Whitely Coggeshall, 1880-1911, Accession Number: 48-2, 8-M239, 2012.

Stanton, Anna, *My Autobiography*, Bishard Brothers, Printers, Des Moines, IA, 1908.

The Des Moines Register, Archives, November 10, 1920, Des Moines, IA.

The Des Moines Register, "Women's Edition of the Register and Leader," May 12, 1915, Des Moines, IA.

The History of Des Moines and Polk County, Vol. 1, S.J. Clark Publishing Co., 1911.

U.S. Quaker Meeting Records, 1681-1935, *Ancestry.*

Wikipedia, "Anna Howard Shaw,"
https://wikipedia.org/wiki/Anna_Howard_Shaw

Wikipedia, "Carrie Chapman Catt,"
https://en.wikipedia.org/wiki/Carrie_Chapman_Catt

Wikipedia, "Catharine Waugh McCulloch,"
https://en.wikipedia.org/wiki/Catherine_Waugh_McCulloch

Wikipedia, "Cornelia Hancock,"
https://en.wikipedia.org/wiki/Cornelia_Hancock

Wikipedia, "Earlham College,"
https://en.wikipedia.org/wiki/Earlham_College

Wikipedia, "Lucretia Mott,"
https://en.wikipedia.org/wiki/Lucretia_Mott

Wikipedia, "Quakers,"
https://en.wikipedia.org/wiki/Quakers

Wikipedia, "Seneca Falls Convention,"
https://en.wikipedia.org/wiki/Seneca_Falls_Convention#Quaker_influence

Wikipedia, "Timeline of women's suffrage in the United States,"
https://en.wikipedia.org/wiki/Timeline_of_women's_suffrage_in_the_United_States

Wikipedia, "Women's suffrage in the United States,"
https://en.wikipedia.org/wiki/Women's_suffrage_in_the_United_States